AF580355

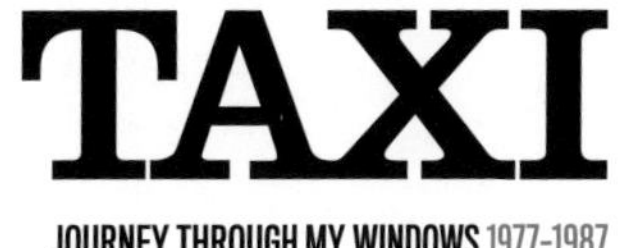
TAXI
JOURNEY THROUGH MY WINDOWS 1977-1987

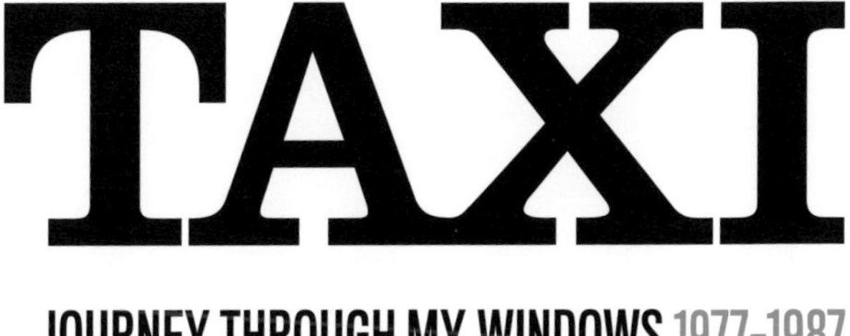

JOURNEY THROUGH MY WINDOWS 1977–1987

PHOTOGRAPHS BY **JOSEPH RODRIGUEZ**   ESSAY BY **RICHARD PRICE**

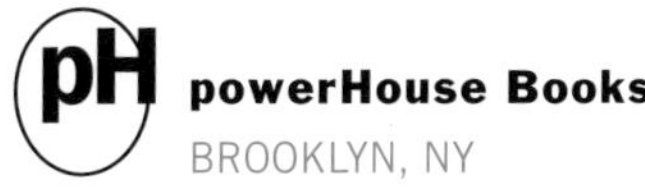

This is an after-after-hours club that was right across from the Film Forum. This place stayed open from like five in the morning to five in the afternoon. It was where you went after the big S&M clubs in the Meatpacking District—Anvil, Hellfire—closed. Back when Al Pacino was doing his research for the film *Cruising*, he would walk in this neighborhood. You would queue up and wait outside this place like the airport.

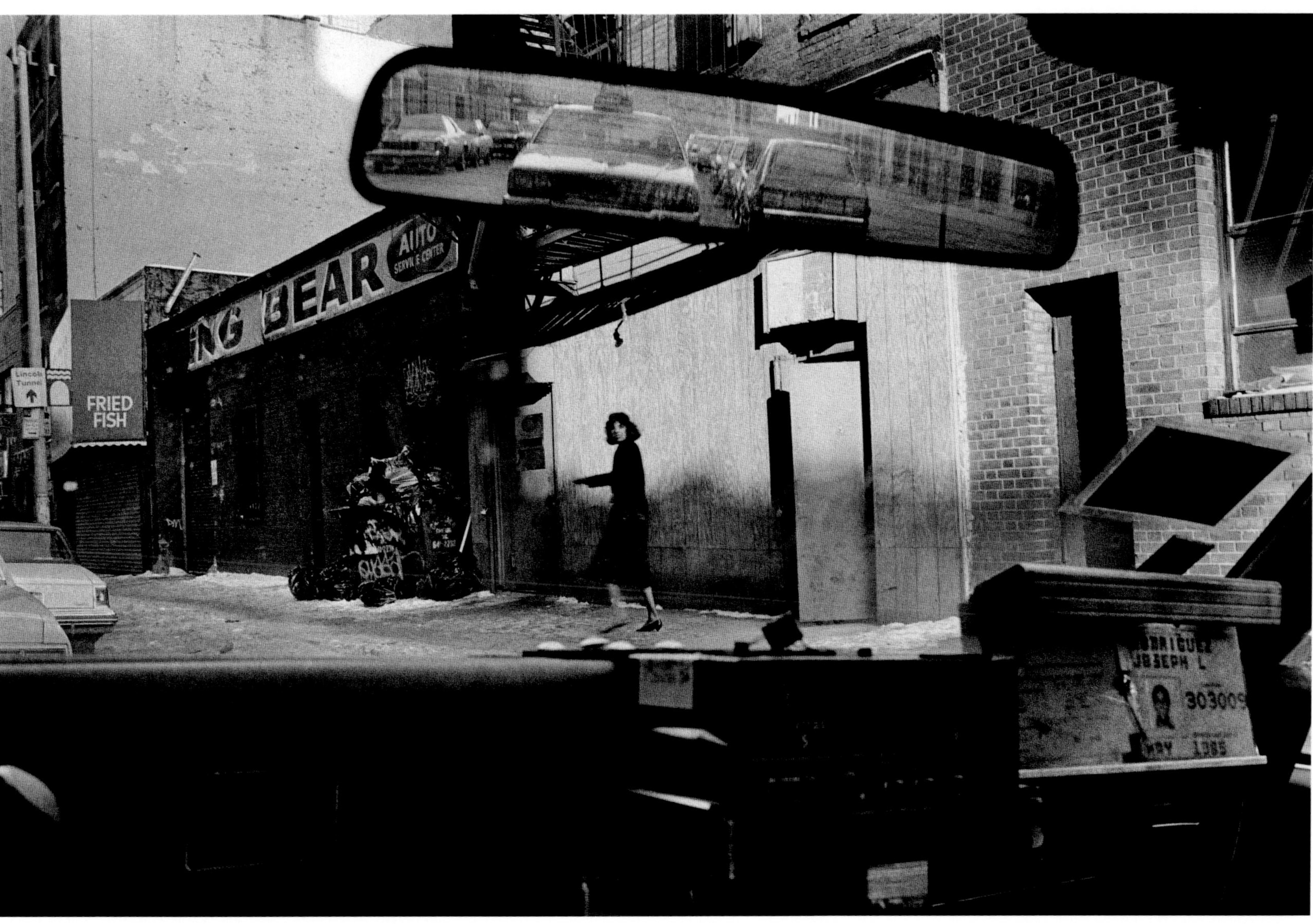
ING BEAR
AUTO
FRIED
FISH
Lincoln
Tunnel
JOSEPH L

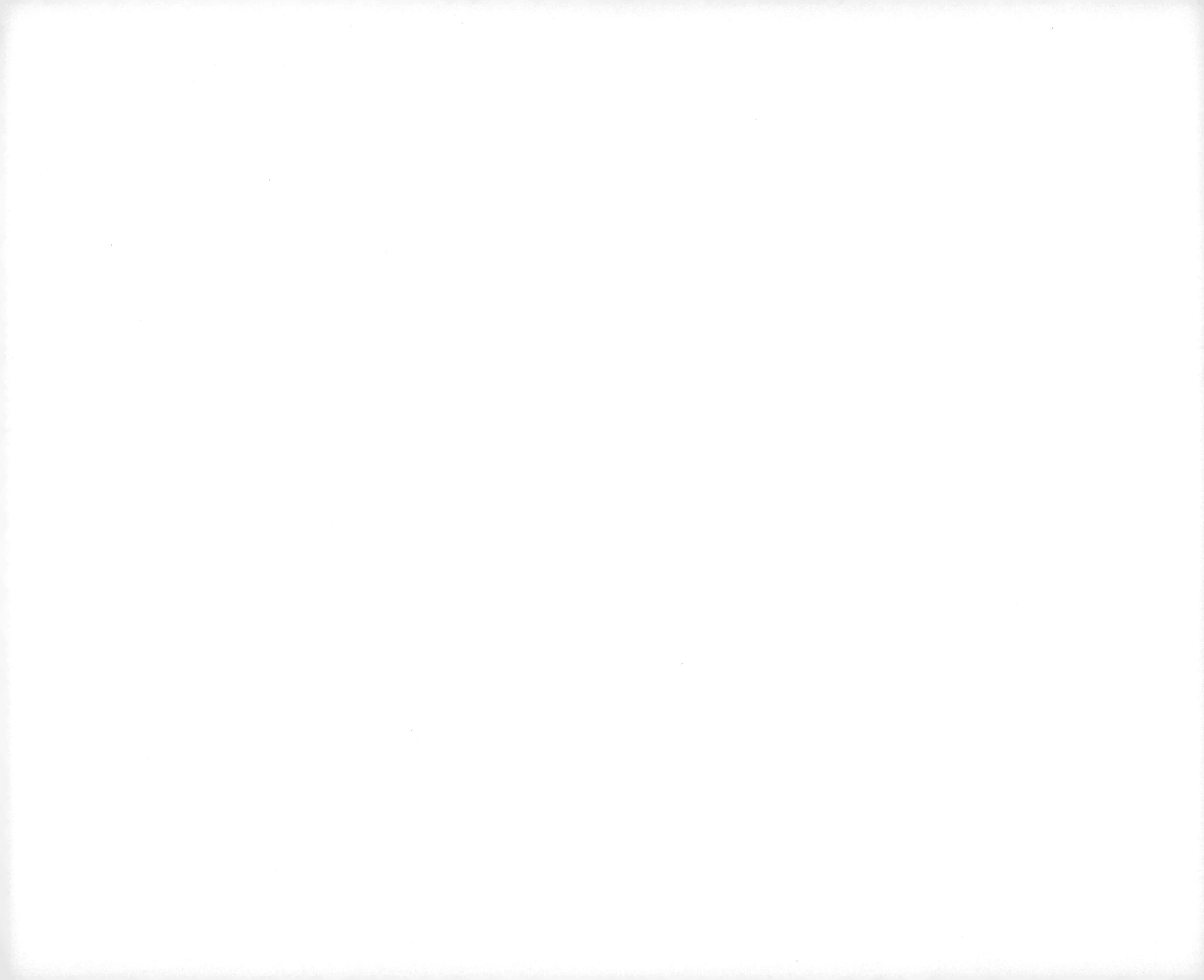

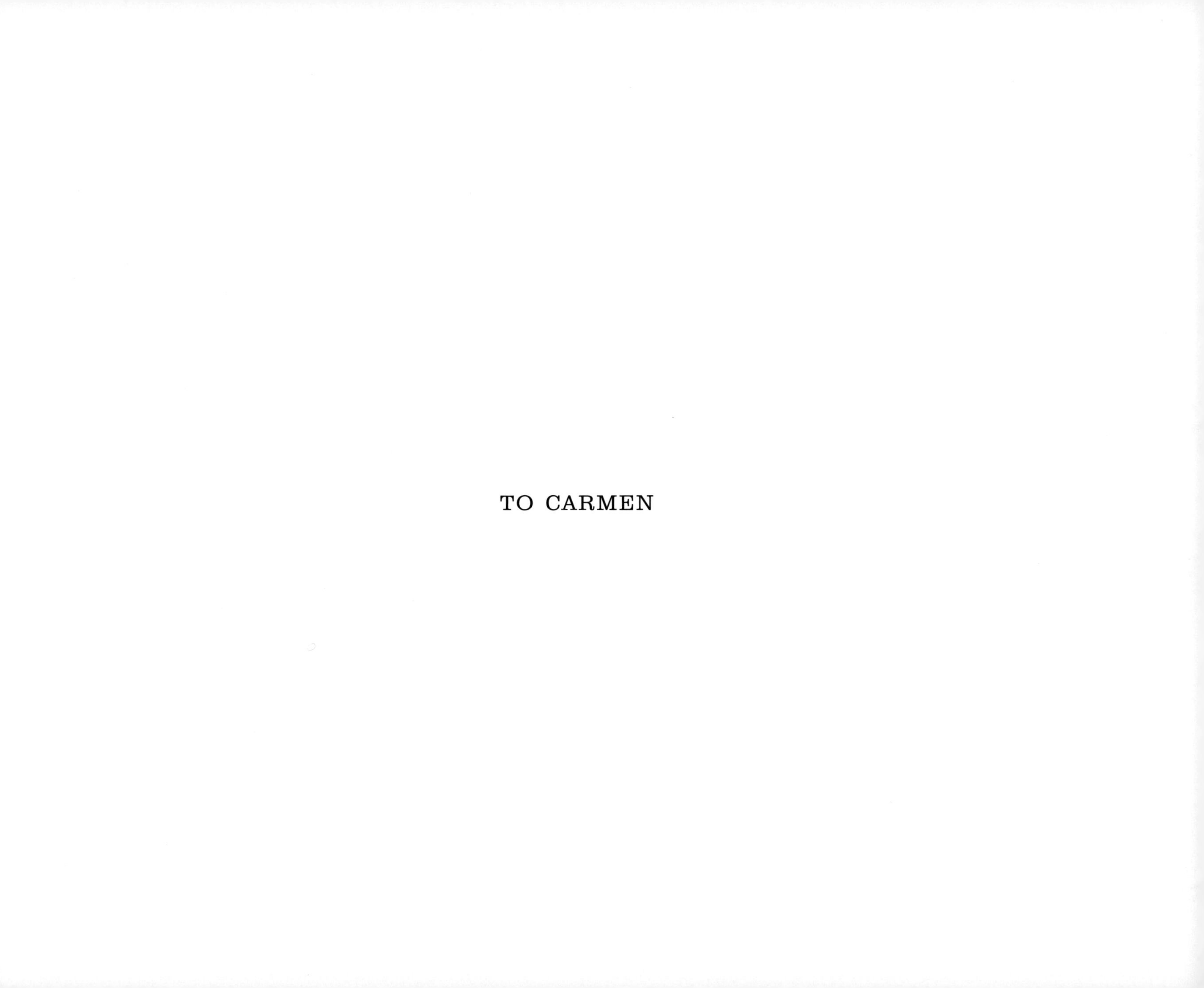

TO CARMEN

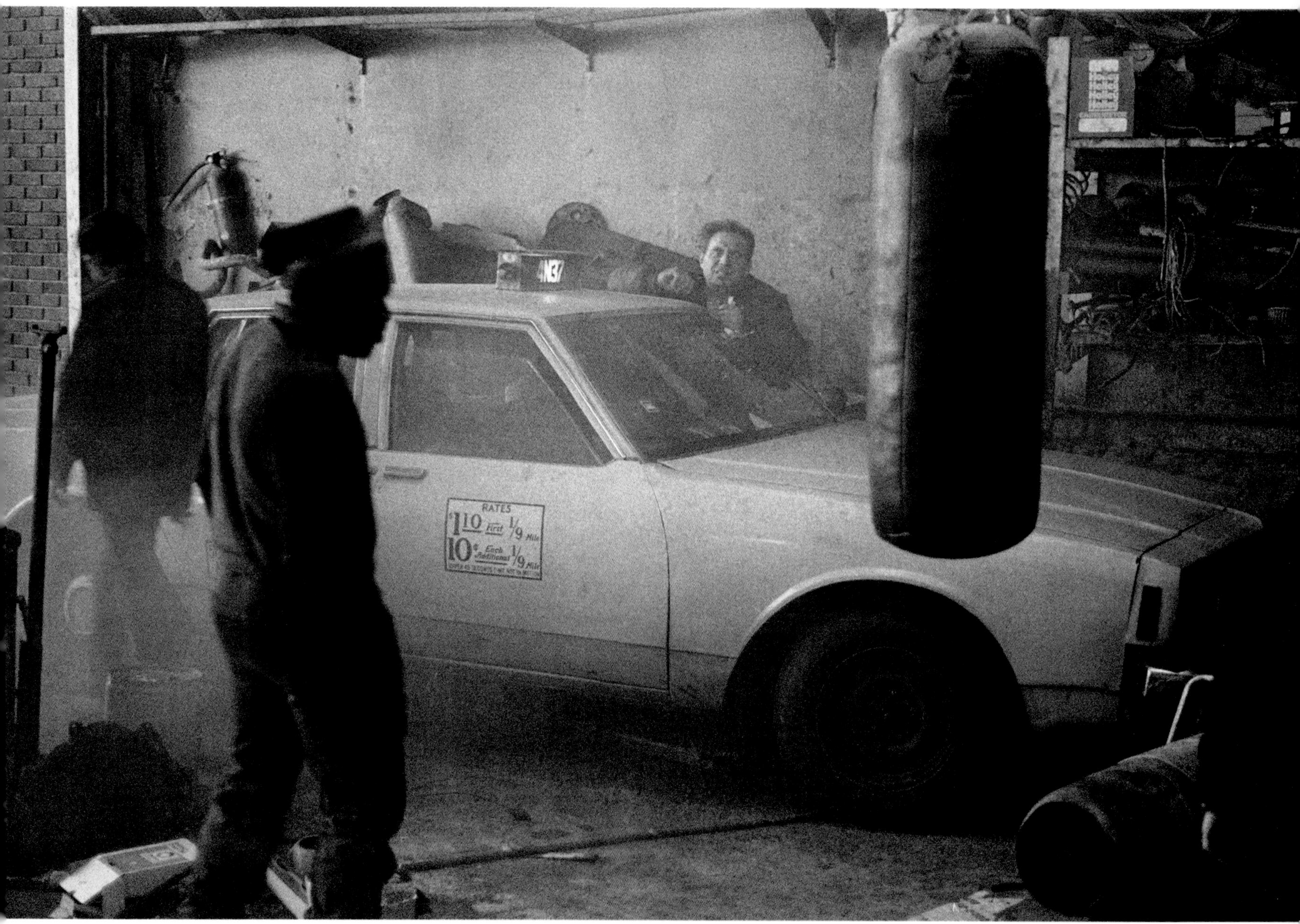
4N37
RATES
$1.10 First 1/9 Mile
10¢ Each Additional 1/9 Mile

FALSE DAWN

THE WEE HOURS HUMANISM OF JOSEPH RODRIGUEZ

By Richard Price

WHEN I THINK BACK on what it was like to live in NYC from 1978 to 1987, the first thing that comes to mind is the old Chinese curse, "May you live in interesting times."

In that ten-year span, it felt like the city was getting its teeth kicked in on a daily basis, encompassing as it did, the dawn and high noon of the AIDS crisis, one municipal budget crisis after another leading to wage and hiring freezes, labor strikes, and in general, an overall deterioration both physical and spiritual in the everyday quality of life.

Street crime was off the hook, cocaine turf wars raged, and, by the mid to late 1980s, the prevalence of crack—a nihilistic WMD if there ever was one—had begun to impose its own brand of devastation on a city already hip-deep in trauma.

To drive a cab back then, you either had to have a death wish or come to the job with a biography that inured you to the danger or graced you with such intuitive empathy/curiosity that to see and hear and sometimes engage with the cavalcade of humanity sliding in and out of your back-seat trumped the nightly game of Russian roulette.

And there was this...

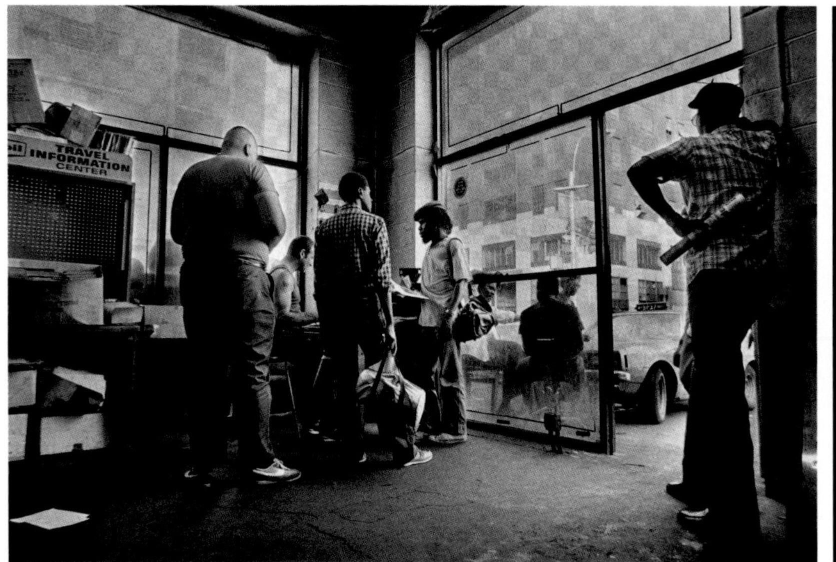

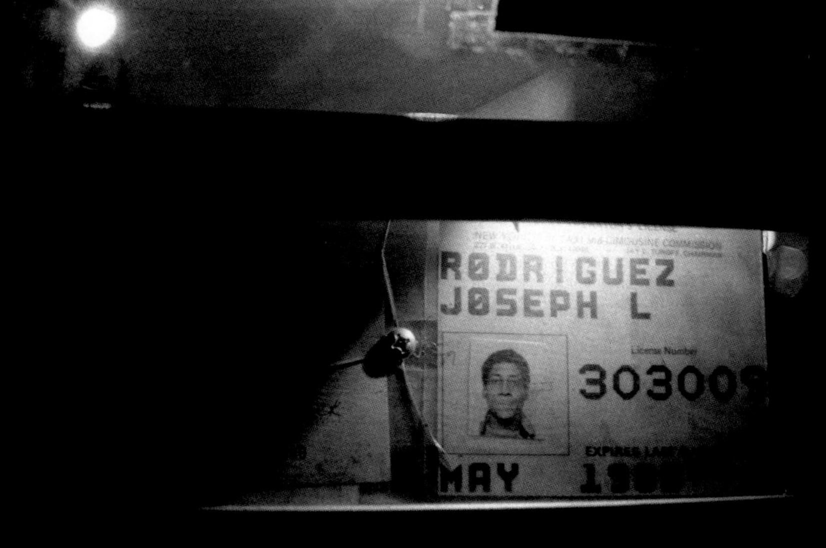

A friend of mine who drove a cab during those years told me about picking up a young couple outside of a Downtown club in the post-midnight hours one night and being directed to drive up and down the West Side Highway from the Brooklyn Battery Tunnel to the George Washington Bridge until his passengers had finished servicing each other in the back seat, then drop them off where he originally picked them up. Returning to the line of waiting hacks in front of the club, his next fare, 30 minutes later, was the same woman with another man, apparently the boyfriend of record…

After giving the driver an address on the Upper East Side, the boyfriend immediately began complaining about spending an hour looking all over the club for her and demanding to know where she'd been hiding. Over the course of the trip, the girlfriend made occasional rear view mirror eye contact with the driver, but his face apparently didn't register until they arrived at the destination. As the couple headed for their building, she stopped short, then returned to the cab, gesturing for the driver to roll down his window. After studying his face full on for a long moment, she finally asked, "Have we met before?"

To drive a cab in New York City, then as now, is to become invisible. Ensconced in the back seat, separated from you by the glass security partition, your fares, unless wanting to engage, cease to think of you except as a navigational tool; a link between the steering wheel, breaks, and gas pedal.

But if you're of a certain cast of mind, rather than feel dehumanized by that dynamic, you can embrace that invisibility to continuously school yourself on the infinite varieties of human experience.

And if in addition to that, you happened to be a socially oriented visual artist…

LIKE ALL THE GREAT social documentarians from Jacob Riis to Lewis Hine to Dorothea Lange, Walker Evans and Helen Levitt, the overarching mission of Joseph Rodriguez's work is to make visible those we choose not to see: the shunned, the ignored, the demonized. In short, to confront us with the everyday humanity of the underclass *Other*.

Much social documentary work tends to focus on the impact of an ongoing event or situation on a specific economic or cultural class—a mass migration, an exploited workforce, the lives of people caught in the deadly crossfire between political/warring powers beyond their control—and in some dire cases, to record for future generations the last notes from home of a people on the verge of annihilation.

In nearly all of his previous work, Rodriguez has remained within the physical boundaries of his subject's world; immersing himself in the life of gang families in East Los Angeles; in the life of everyday people in the war zones of Afghanistan and Pakistan; in the lives of youthful offenders caught up in the machinery of the juvenile justice system. However, in this book, the cab makes him a rover, requiring him in the course of his 4:00 A.M. to 4:00 P.M. shifts to find subjects wherever he's directed to go.

Some of the most powerful images in here are those of his first fares; the lone hustlers, sex workers, cross-dressers, and last-call leather bar patrons as they wrap it up in the existential zero hour between the end of night and the colorless first light of day. From portrait to portrait, he captures these people in all their emotional complexity; their defiance and their weariness, their dream-selves and their fatalism.

Surprisingly, for a street photographer whose work can brim with physical vitality, there's also a great amount of monkish contemplation to be found here; the earliest hours of his shift offer him the mute beauty of a rising sun striking the high floors of a skyscraper before slowly making its way down to the shadowed street, or of a major bridge in its misty pre-dawn repose before bearing the onslaught of the day's swarming traffic. In other of these depopulated still lifes, he captures not the peace of these places, but the sense of utter abandonment, as if the absence of people is permanent and what we're encountering is the abject leavings of a lost civilization.

STYLISTICALLY, **RODRIGUEZ** can be as narratively frank as any of the politically charged New York Photo League street shooters of the 1930s, 40s, and 50s — some of his people look into the camera while holding up handwritten messages scrawled on cardboard as if to provide their own photo captions — or as jaggedly suggestive as Vivian Maier; rendering his people as shadows, silhouettes, in near-abstract streaks of motion, or reduced in their passed out oblivion to a pile of clothing on the sidewalk lying there in brutal juxtaposition to the hectic clip of those who pass by.

If Rodriguez's artistic mission is to evoke, through empathy, both pity for, and outrage at the plight of others, one of the more effective strategies he employs is to work against the grain of suffering to capture the everyday joys that even the most afflicted communities have

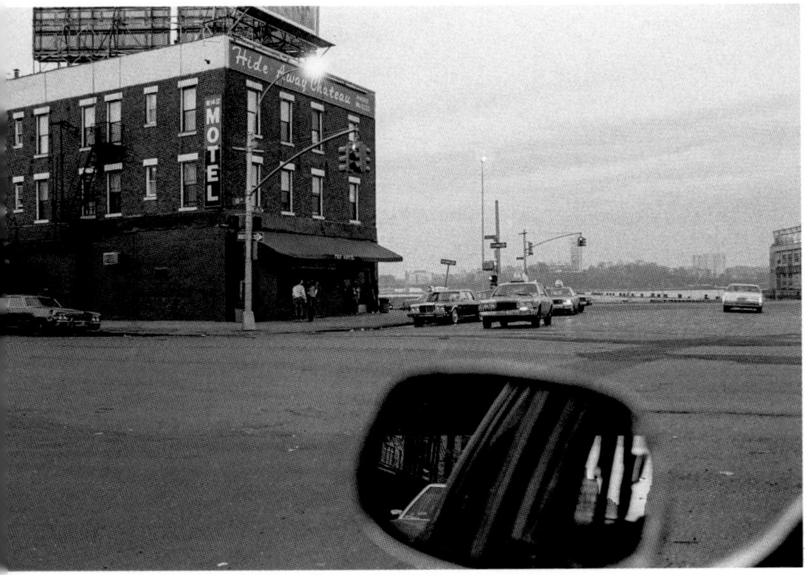

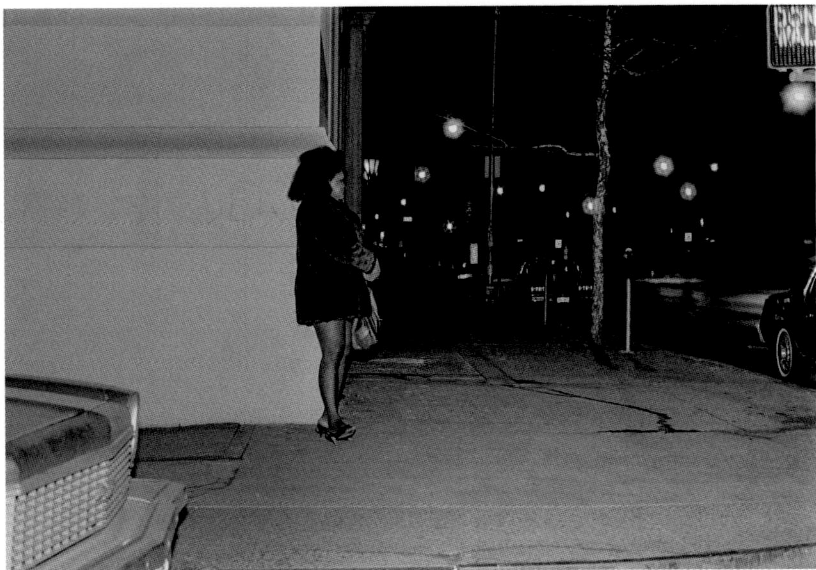

been blessed with; the camaraderie of the street, the deep multi-generational ties of families, the succors of home, the small and large ceremonies that celebrate the various rites of passage in a person's life.

There is a great sense of humility in these images; a sense that the artist in the more ragged moments of his own life, or even now, could just as easily stand before his own camera as behind it.

In the end, it all comes down to this—that in order to be a great street photographer, you need to love the street.

And as evident in *Taxi*, nobody understands or expresses this better than Joseph Rodriguez.

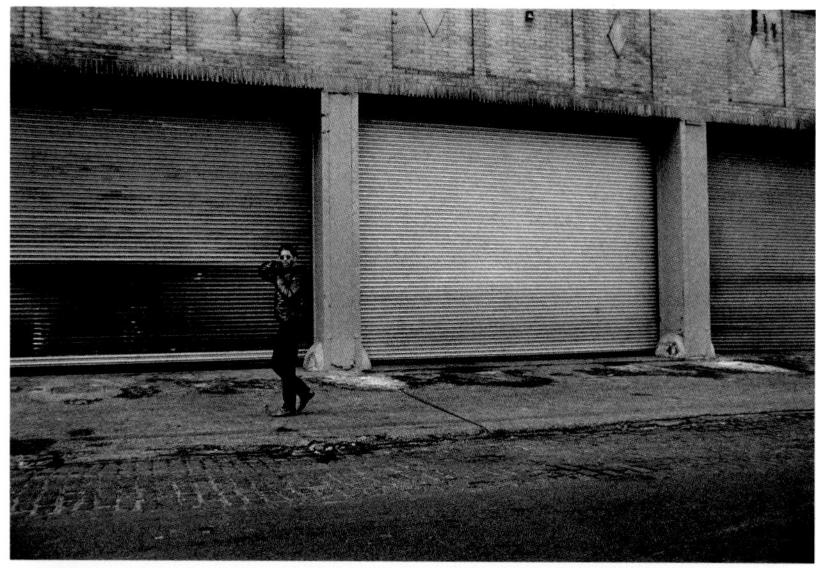

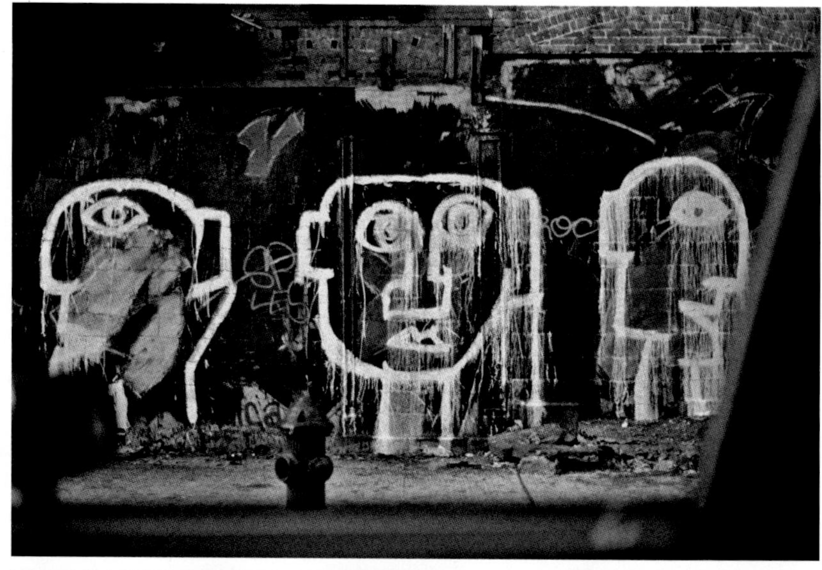

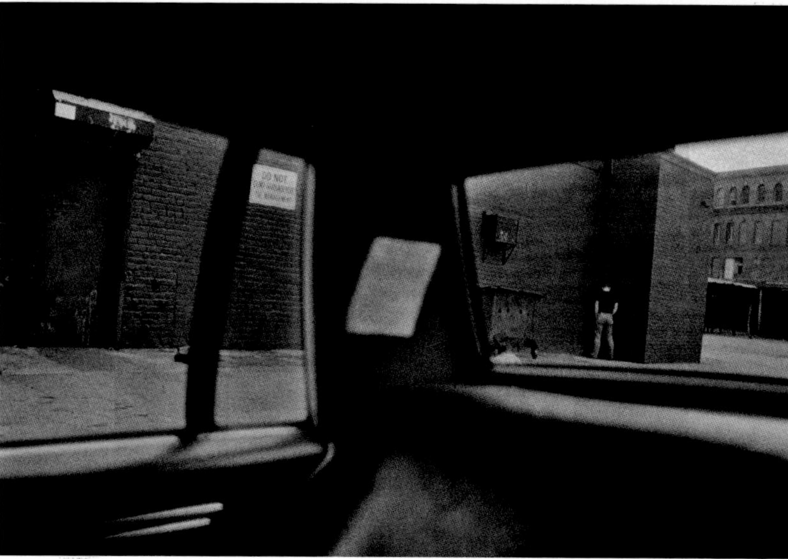
DO NOT

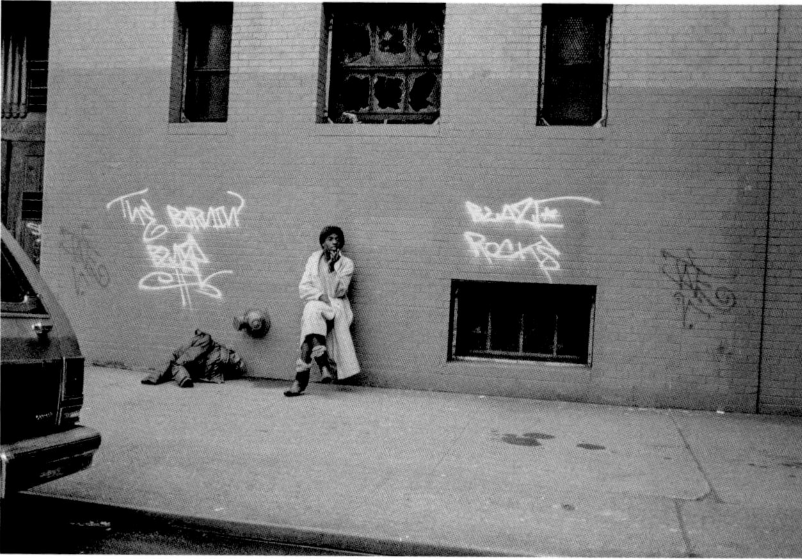

TAXI JOURNAL

SUNDAY MORNING. My shift starts at 5:00 a.m. I'm hoping for a good cab—sometimes you get a real piece of junk. That's the way it is when you don't have a steady cab. You lease one for $60 per 12-hour shift, plus gas. I take several minutes to check out the cab—I'll be in this yellow box all day.

I pull out of the garage, and the race begins—looking for fares. I know that the after-hours clubs might be jumping, so I cruise by the Hellfire, an S&M club notorious for its wild stage acts. I pull up to the door and wait for a passenger.

A fare approaches. She is wearing a cabaret outfit in high heels and asks, "Will you take me to Brooklyn?" "Where in Brooklyn?" I respond. "Bushwick, take the Williamsburg Bridge," she says. I hit the meter, and we're on our way. Driving down Broadway, I ask my fare how her night performing was—did she make money? She nods and says, "It was OK... but you know it's a bitch to make living these days." We talk for a bit and then I ask if I can take her photograph. I tell her that I'm working on a book. We talk a little more; finally we arrive at a tenement on Chauncey Street. She pays the fare, plus a tip. As I begin cruising back over the bridge to Manhattan the sun is coming up over the city, a wonderful view. I slow down to take a quick photo. I deeply appreciate the feelings of peace and isolation. In a few hours the streets will be flourishing with bumper-to-bumper traffic.

I rush back to the City to hustle up a few more fares before the clubs close. I get on the taxi line for the Mineshaft, another S&M club. A fare jumps in—"89th Street and Park Avenue," he says. As we begin to get closer to his Upper East Side destination, I glance in my rearview mirror; he is changing out of his leather outfit (with whip and boots) into a pair of khakis, oxford shirt, and penny loafers. By the time we arrive at his Park Avenue apartment building, he's transformed into a Wall Street banker. The doorman greets him. I say to myself, "There are eight million stories in the Naked City; this has been one of them."

As the other half of the city starts to wake, I cruise by Penn Station for the working commuters. A Black woman gets in. "Where to lady?" I ask. "89th Street and East End Avenue please," she replies in a sweet voice. I ask her what she does for a living; she tells me she is domestic worker cleaning houses for people. "Isn't it something how many people have to work so hard? That's life I guess," she says. I think it is true that every cab driver has compassion for workers like her that do hard jobs.

Cruising back downtown on Second Avenue. I hope to get a fare to the airport, but an old couple flags me down. I get out to help them in; old people are slow, so you must have patience. Suddenly, they fascinate me. I ask how long they have been married. "Forty years," the husband says. I ask how they've managed to live together so long, because lots of marriages do not last that long. They both said "love and compromise" was their belief.

Later, cruising up Broadway a man jumps in. He wants to go to Teaneck, New Jersey. I say, "That is double the meter plus tolls." He begins rapping to me, "You know brother-man, money is the key. It'll make you happy, it gives you power and without it you are lost." I reply, "I hear that." I do not agree, but it is funny how many people buy into it.

Back in Manhattan, I stop to see how much I have made. I count $120. To make a decent wage, I must hustle more fares in the few hours left before my shift ends. The dispatcher dislikes it when I bring in the cab late, for there waits another driver for the night shift. I wonder what kind of fares he will meet.

—Joseph Rodriguez, June 1986

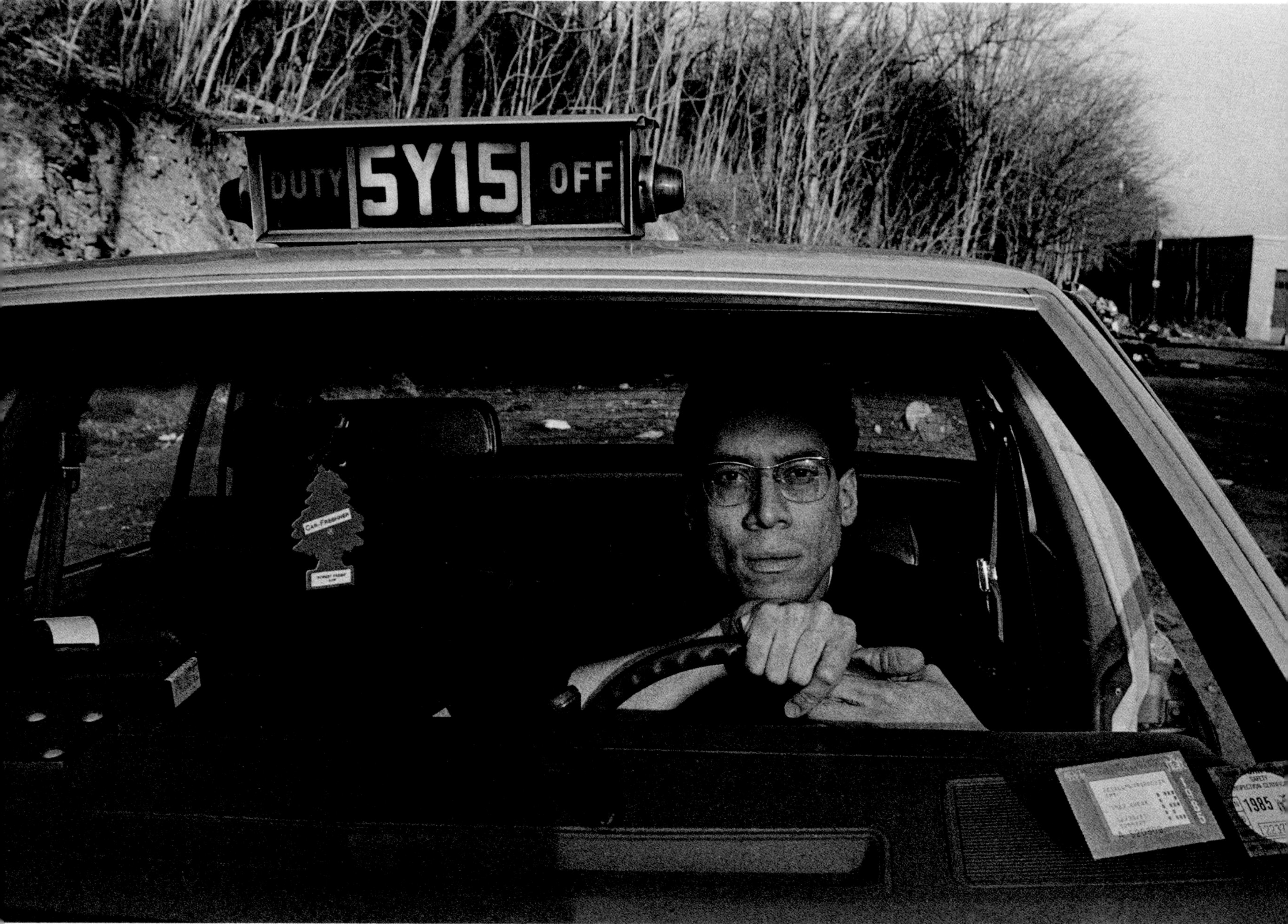
DUTY
5Y15
OFF
CAR-FRESHNER
1985

THE DAY SHIFT was 4:00 A.M. TO 4:00 P.M. If you were a day shift guy, you started out by picking your cab up at four in the morning. By the time you got your cab, commuters started coming into the city and Penn Station had come alive. The hotels would be stirring with people on their way to the airport. This is like five in the morning. You knew the rhythm of the city in terms of traffic. By six, the city is really popping. Grand Central, Port Authority, Hilton Hotel, Downtown, Wall Street—this is all moving now. Then it slows down after nine, ten in the morning, because everyone is at work. Traffic starts to slow down, truck traffic starts to pick up because there are deliveries. Eleven, twelve, it's lunchtime, so there's not much going on, so you go sit in front of a hotel and you hope for a fare to the airport. You want to get out of the city, get to the airport, those are the big fares. You drop somebody off at JFK, you wait a couple hours to bring somebody back. That's the day shift routine.

I STARTED DRIVING IN 1977. There was a lot going on in those two or three years—I got off methadone, I went to Brooklyn Technical College from '78 to '80, got a two year degree. And during that time, I drove.

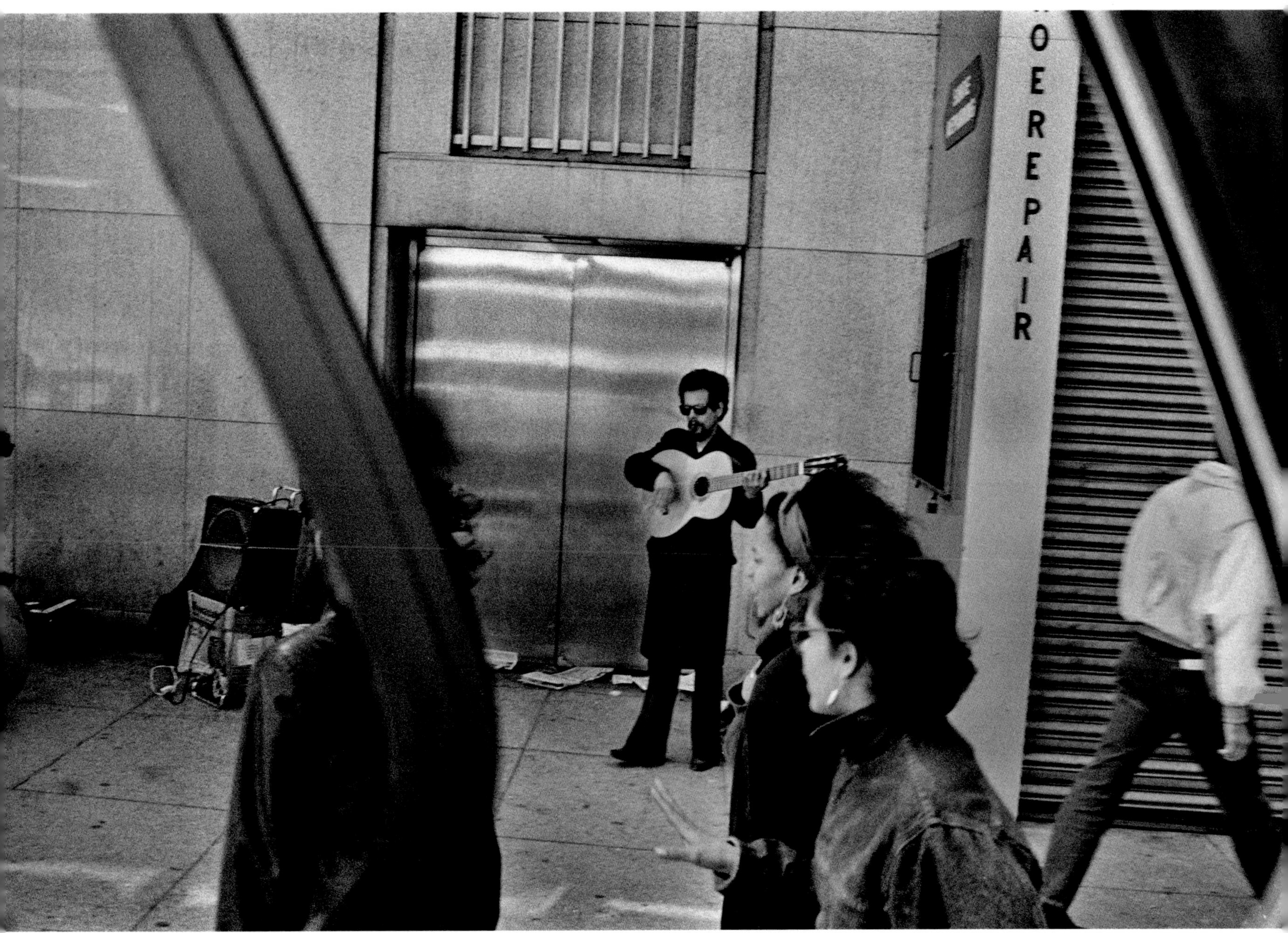
OEREPAIR

I WAS GETTING COFFEE ON 58TH Street, and I saw this Fiorucci model walking down the sidewalk with a stylist. There was a truck full of guys in the street, yelling, "Hey mami, what's up?" and because the guy was looking at her, he runs straight into the car in front of them.

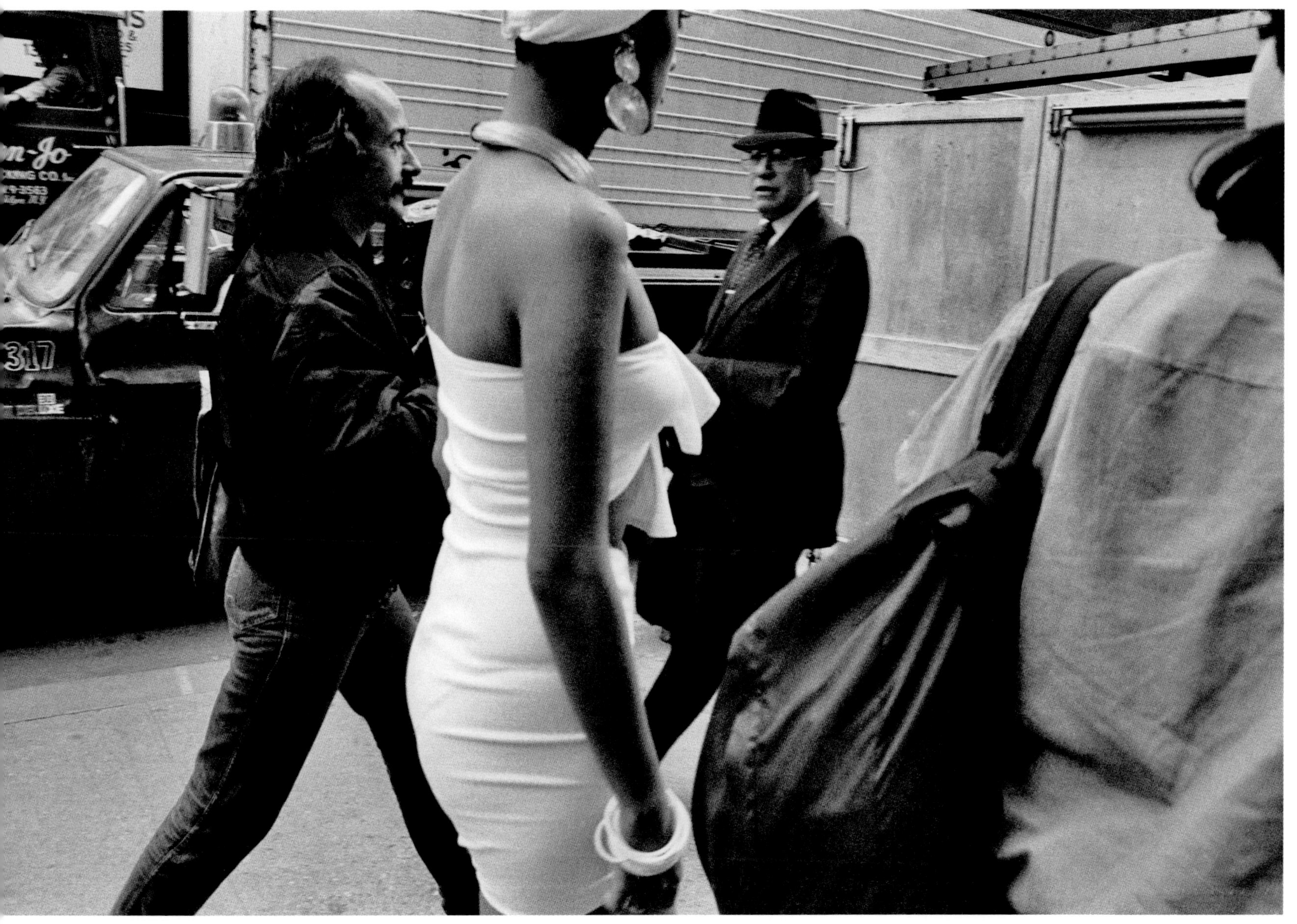
n-Jo
317

I WAS TAKING A WORKSHOP with Mary Ellen Mark at ICP, and I had all these pictures I was taking of the street through the window of the cab. And she really challenged me. She said, “It doesn’t seem that you’re brave enough to take pictures of people in the cab. There are people right next to you. Take pictures of them.” So that was when I started making portraits of my passengers.

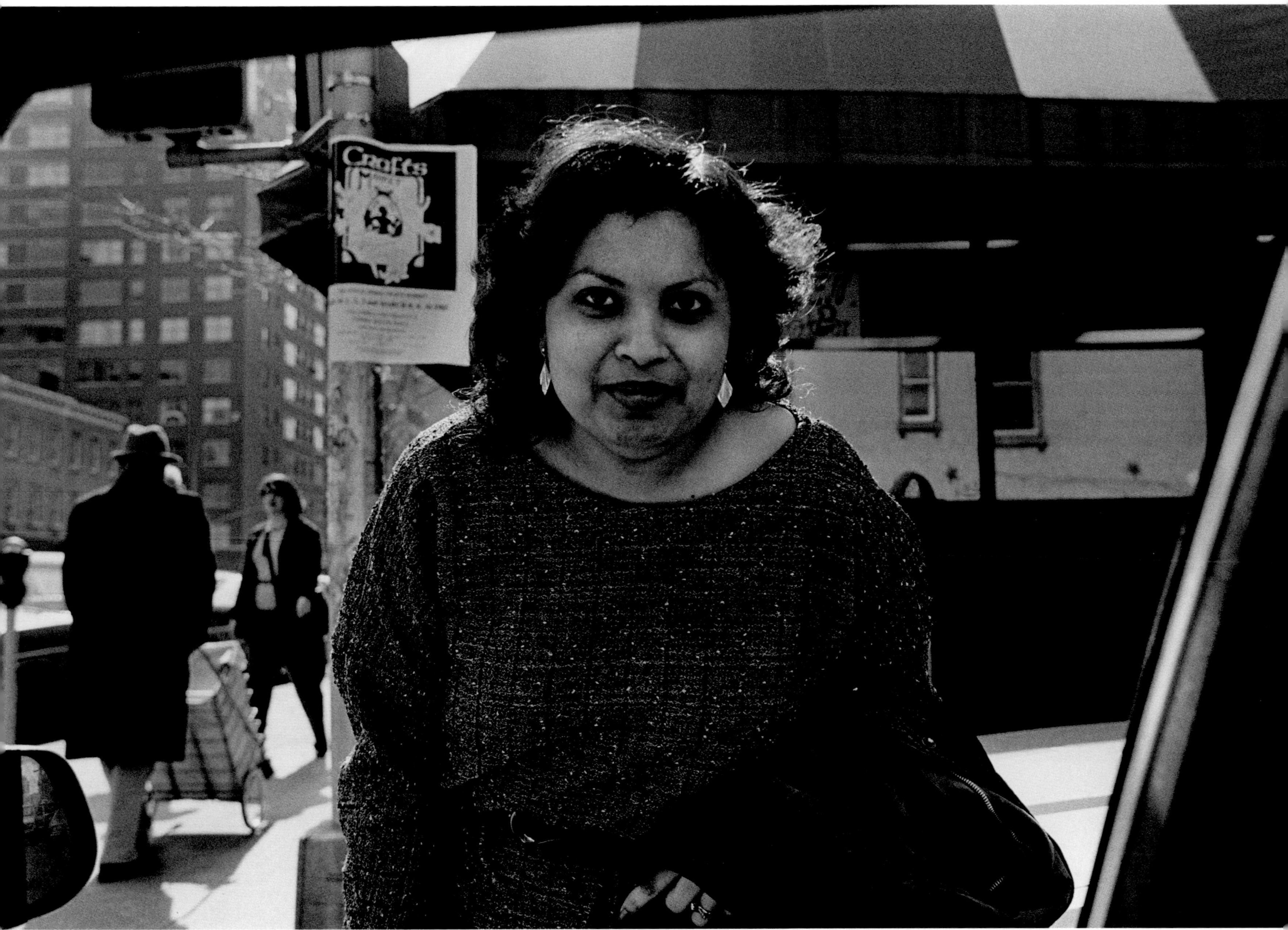
Crafts

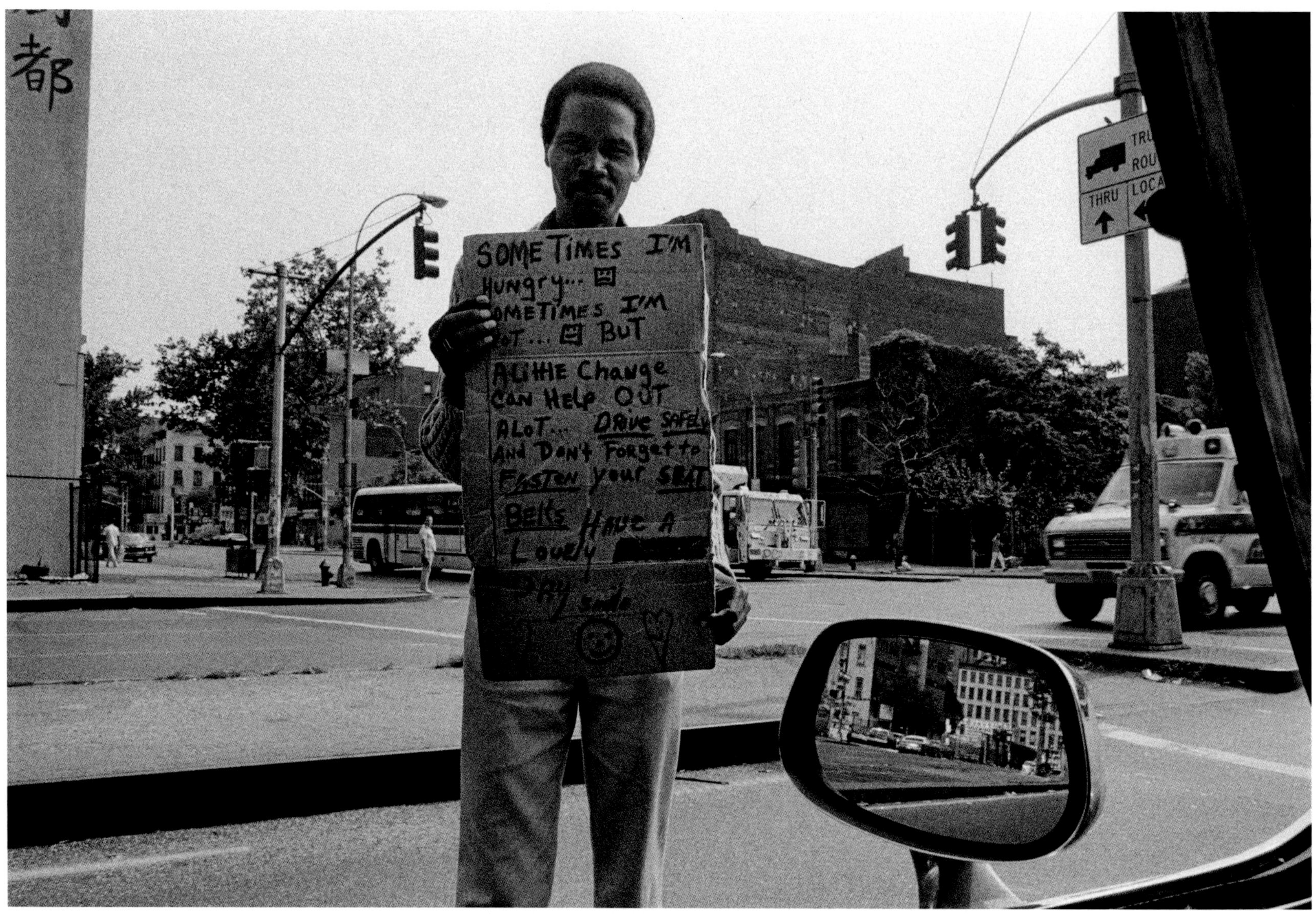

都
SOMETIMES I'M
Hungry...
SOMETIMES I'M
BUT
Alittle Change
Can Help OUT
ALOT... DRIVE SAFELY
And Don't Forget to
Fasten your SEAT
Belts HAVE A
Lovely
THRU

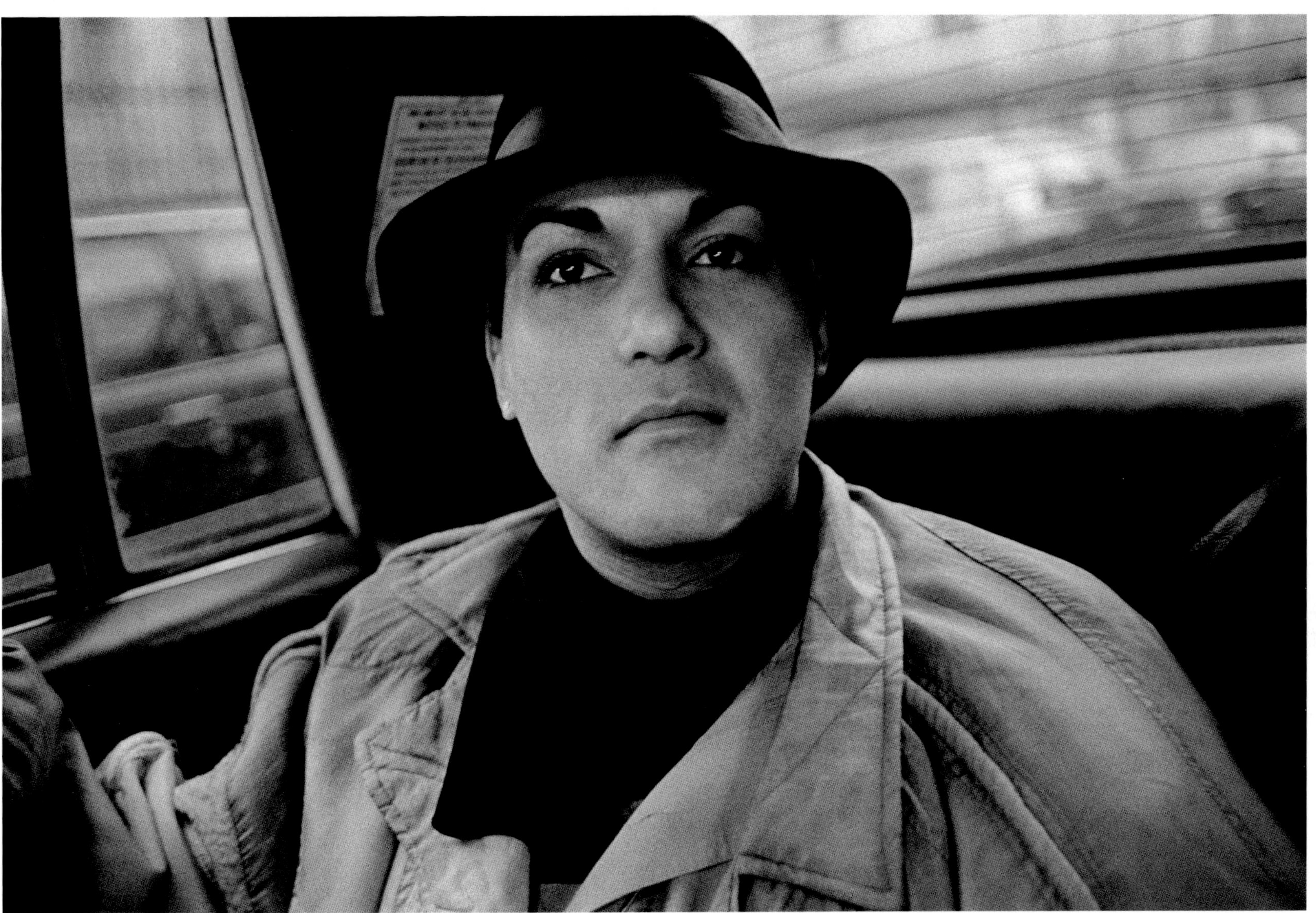

I USED TO DRIVE for this Israeli guy who had a garage on 15TH Street and Ninth Avenue. He would buy used cop cars from highway patrols in New Jersey and Connecticut and paint them yellow. But he was also changing the VIN numbers. I was getting ready to go to work one morning, and I see my boss in the *New York Post*:

"TAXI OWNER CHANGES VIN NUMBERS."

So I get there, and I don't have a job anymore.

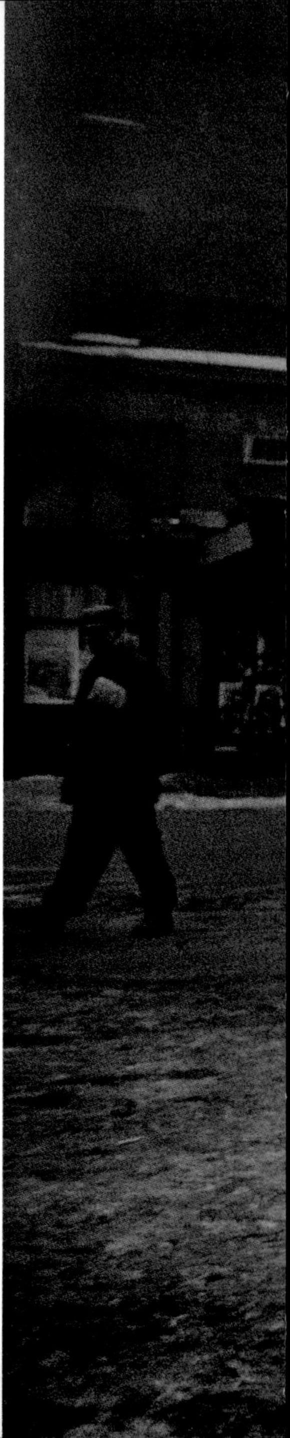

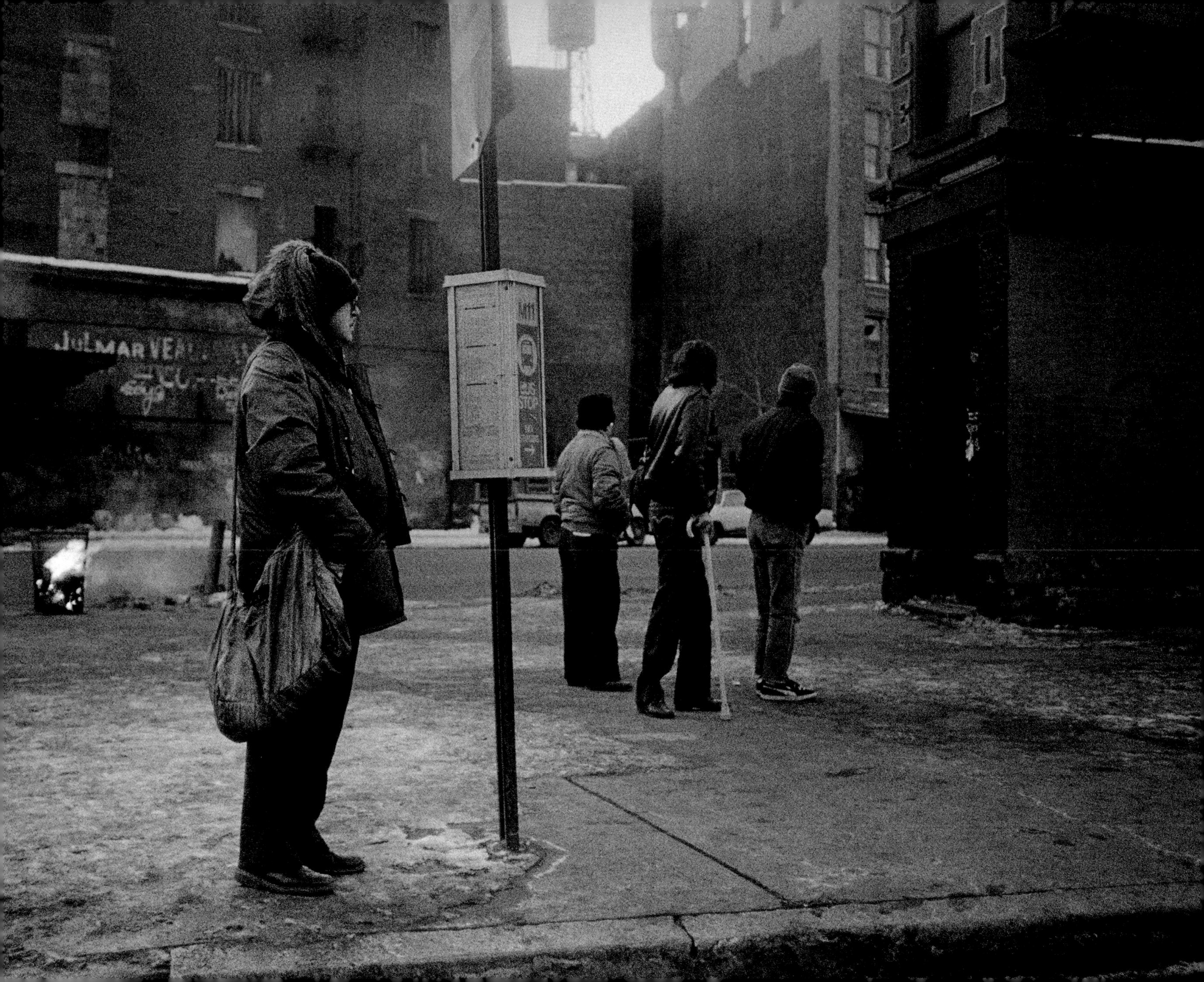
JULMAR
BUS STOP

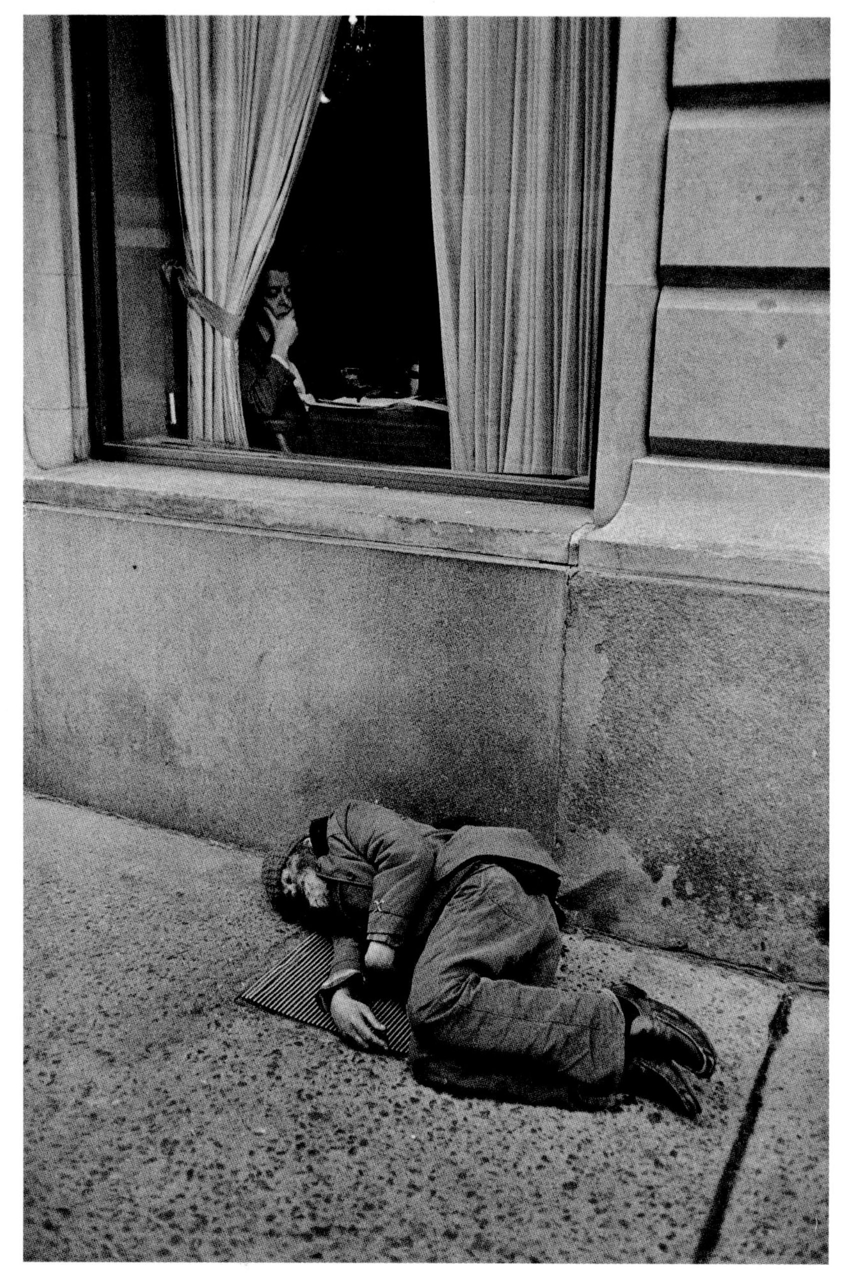

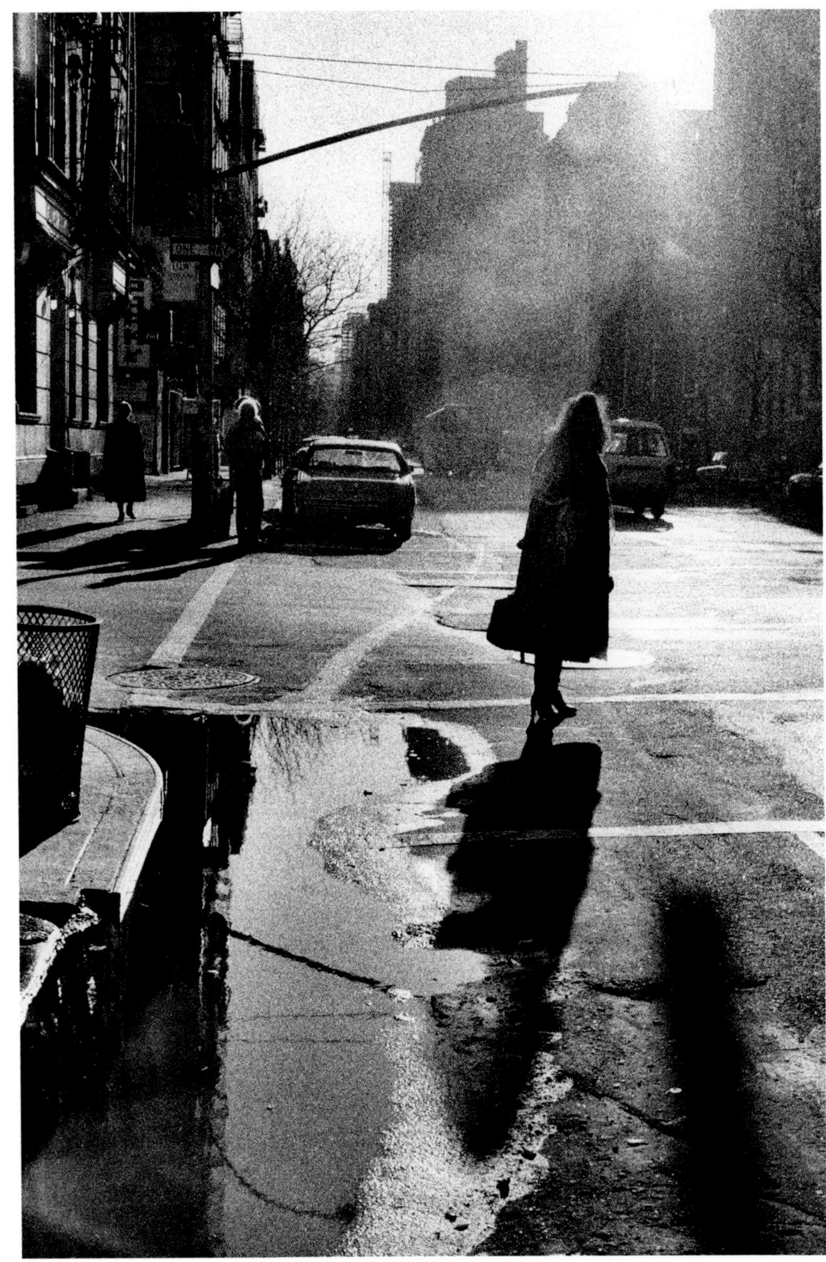

I WAS HAVING a really hard time having a relationship, and I get this couple in my cab who are married 45 years. My question to the both of them was, "How do you stay married for so long?" The man starts complaining about her gas at night, and she was complaining about his snoring. But they agreed their secret was "love and compromise."

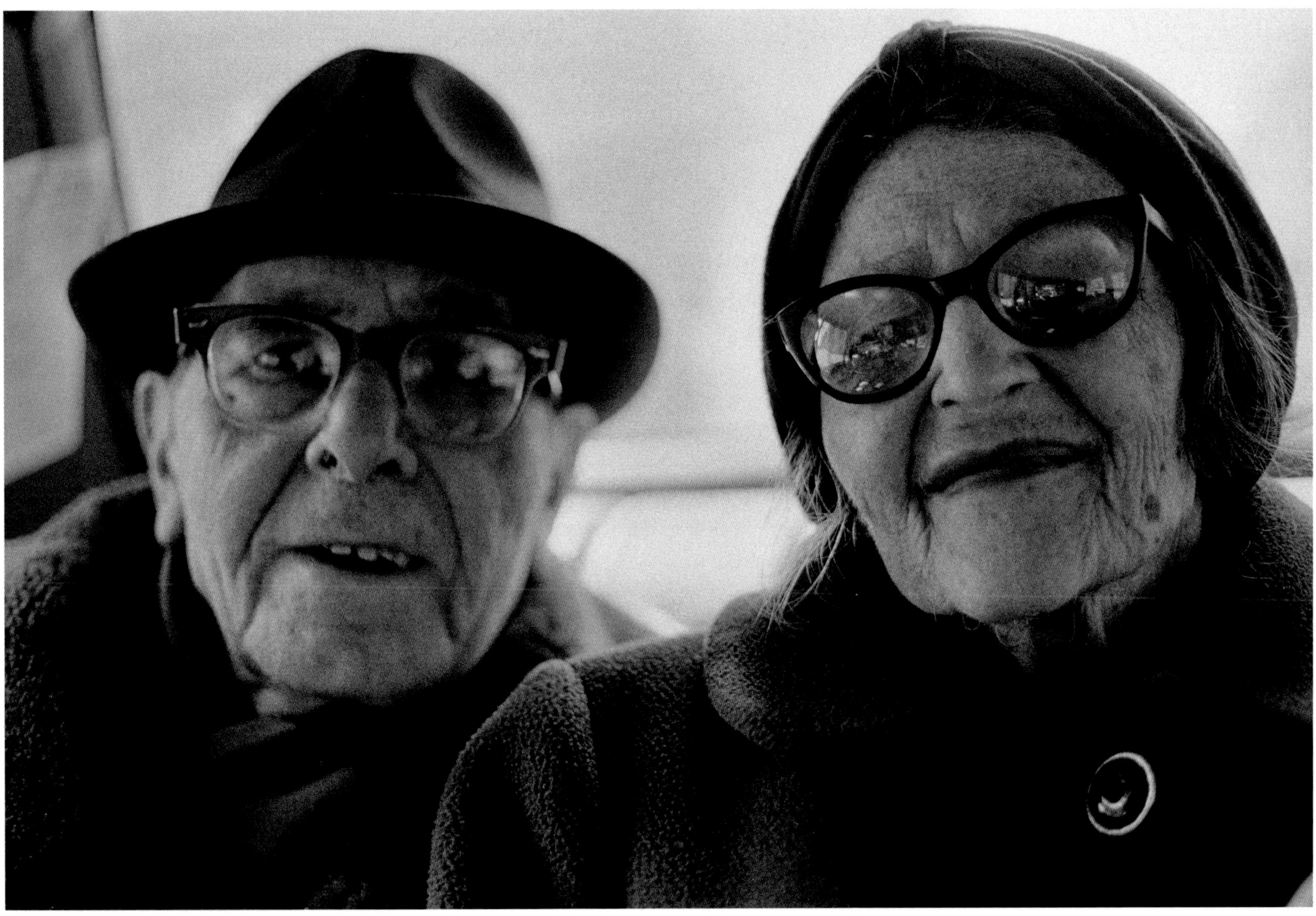

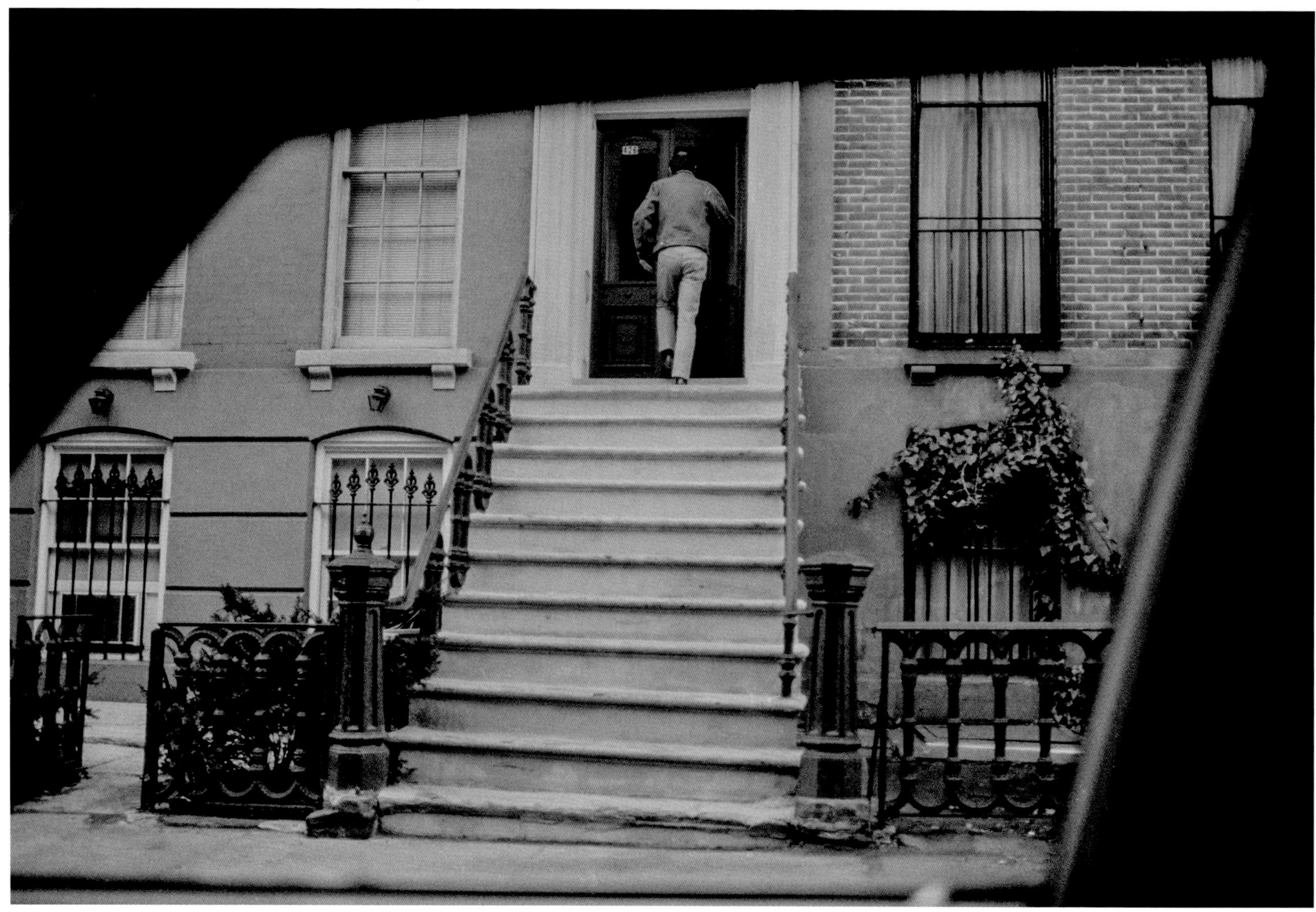

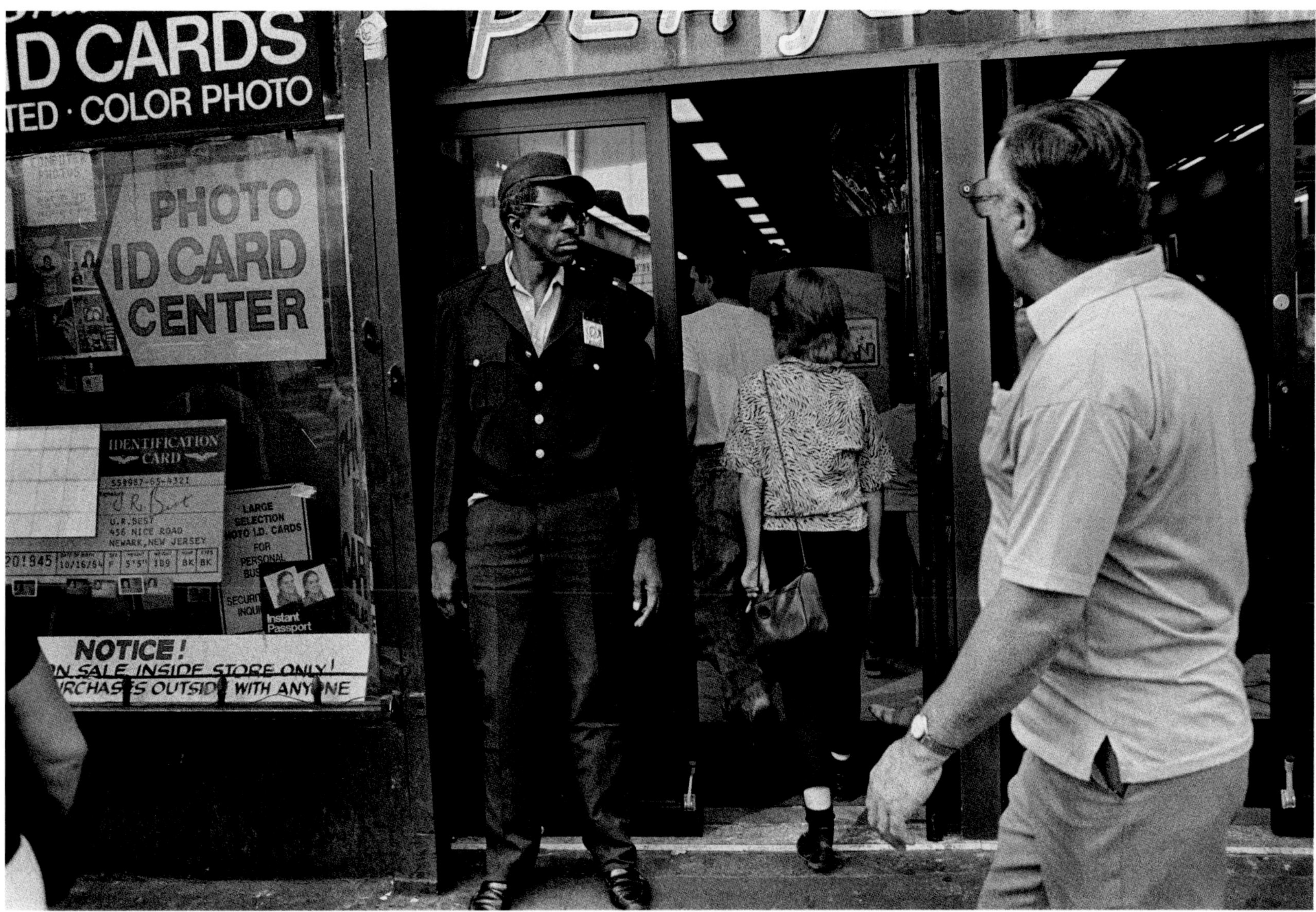
ID CARDS
COLOR PHOTO
PHOTO
ID CARD
CENTER
IDENTIFICATION
CARD
LARGE
SELECTION
FOR
Instant
Passport
NOTICE!

I HAD THIS REGULAR who was a sex worker. I would pick her up all the time around daybreak, and drive her home to Brooklyn. This one night, she gets in the cab, and wants to make a stop to pick up her money stash in some bushes where she'd hidden it. We pull off, and stop at a red light—then from out of nowhere, her pimp jumps in the back seat. He tells me to take them to East New York, near the Pink Houses (a notorious Brooklyn housing project). Then he starts smacking her around, yelling, "Bitch, where's my money?!" I'm driving, trying to stay cool, but then he pulls a knife out. I don't know what's gonna happen. At first she's trying to play it like she didn't make much, then after the knife comes out she gives him the money, quick. I dropped them off, and he paid the fare out of her money. Didn't give me a tip though.

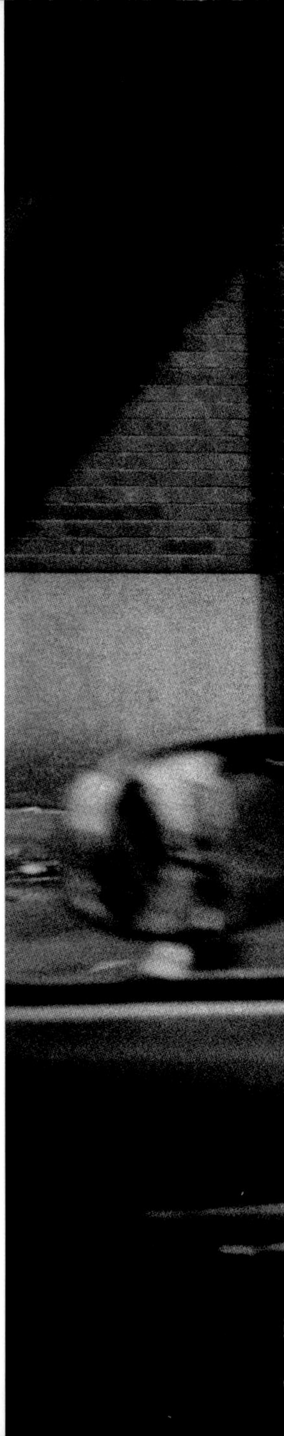

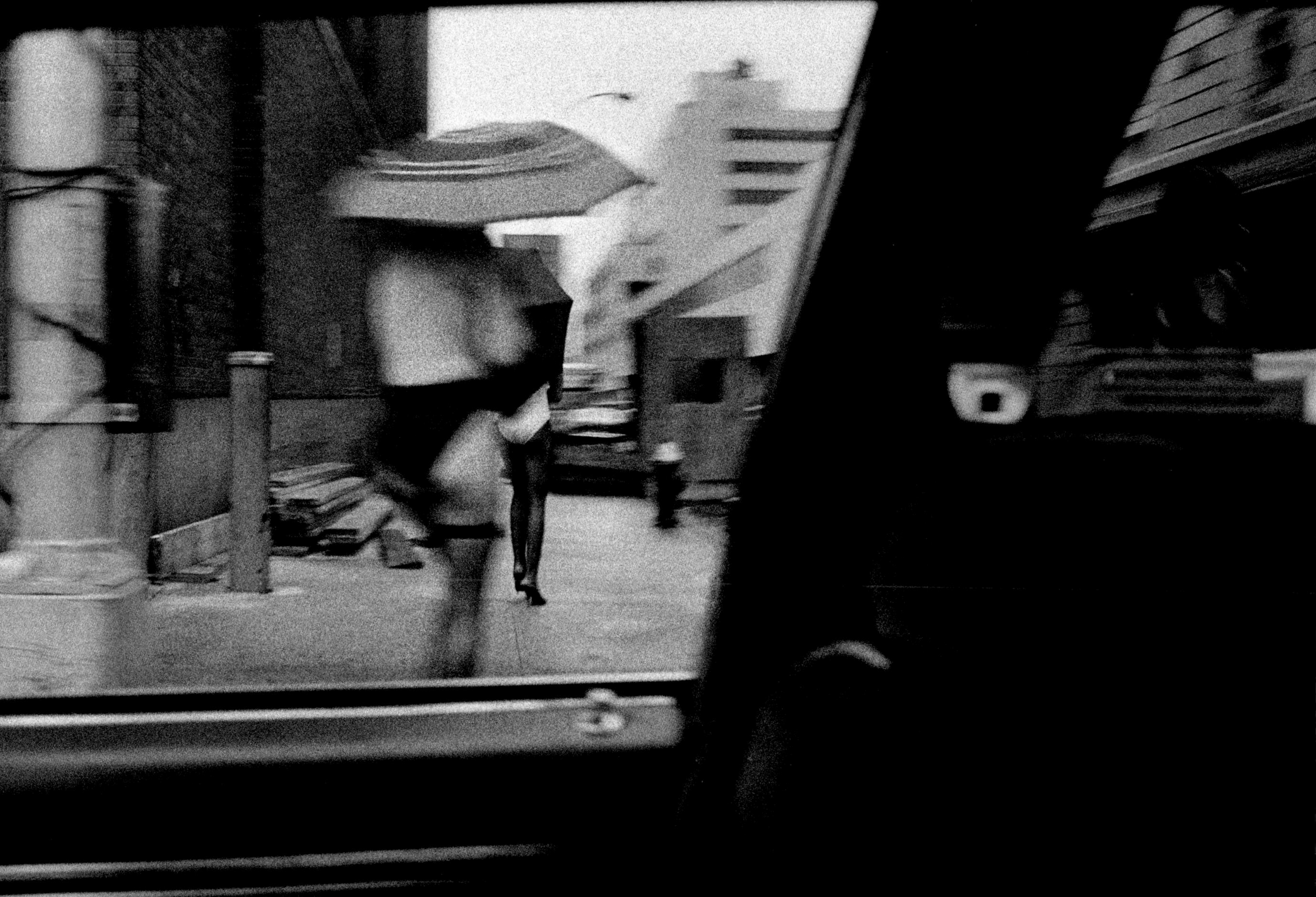

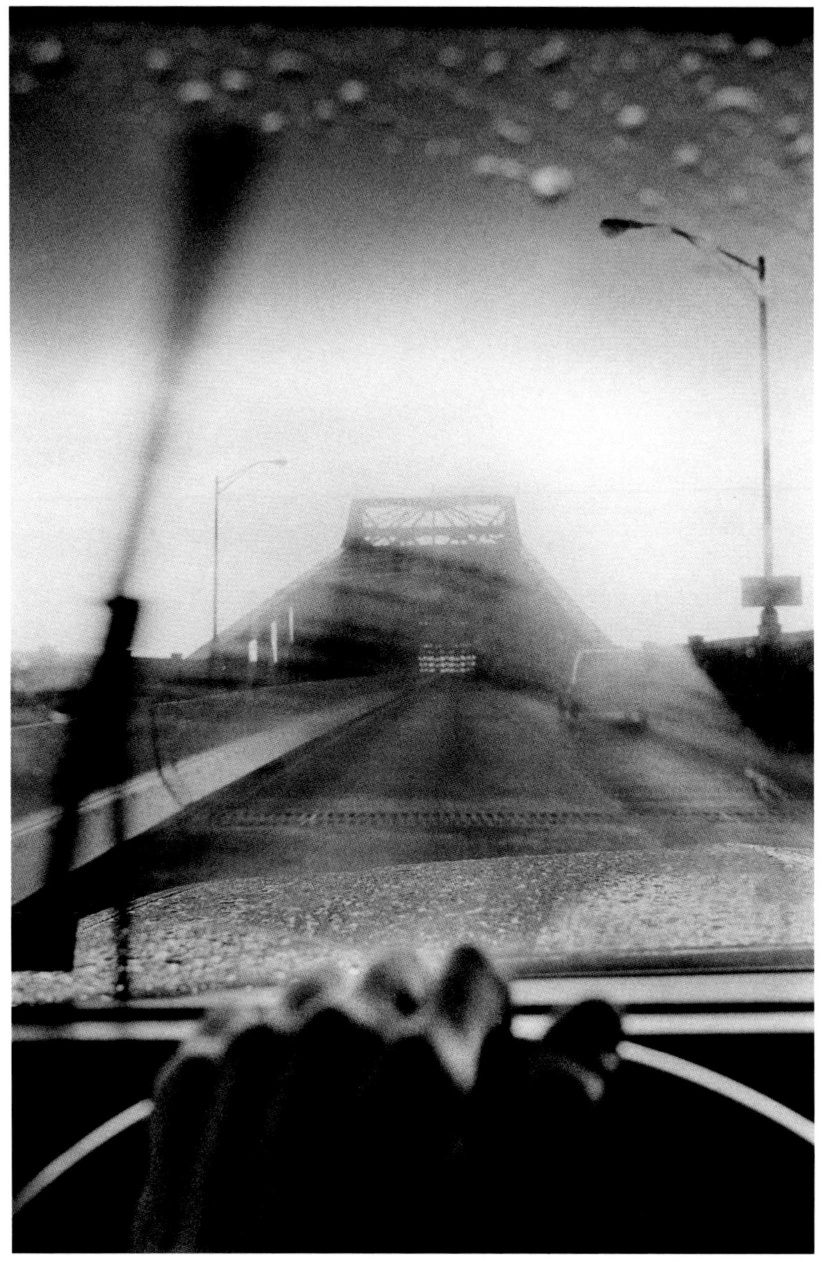

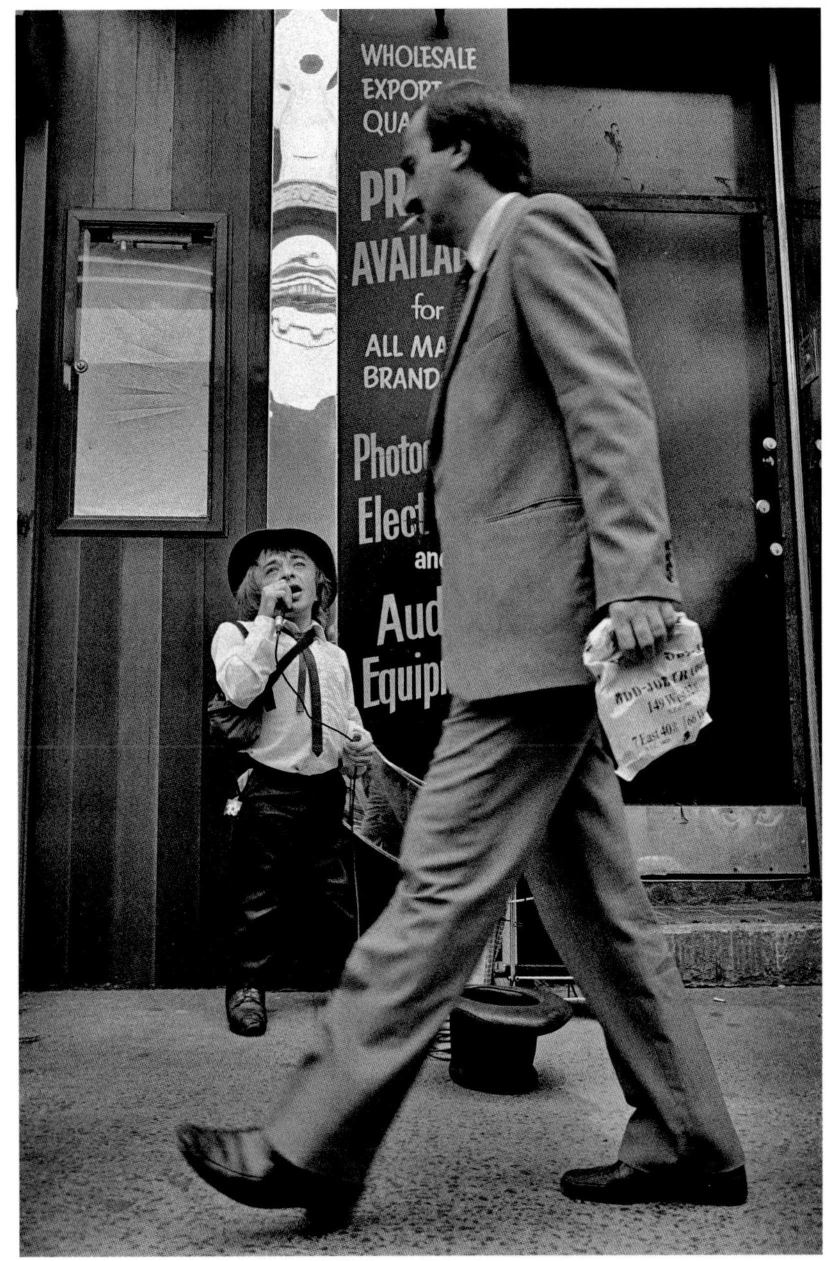
WHOLESALE
EXPORT
for

I HAD BEEN WORKING some of the grittiest clubs all morning on a Sunday. Picking up guys from the Anvil and taking them uptown. And on the way back downtown, there was this family going to church. Smiling little kids, all dressed in their Sunday best.

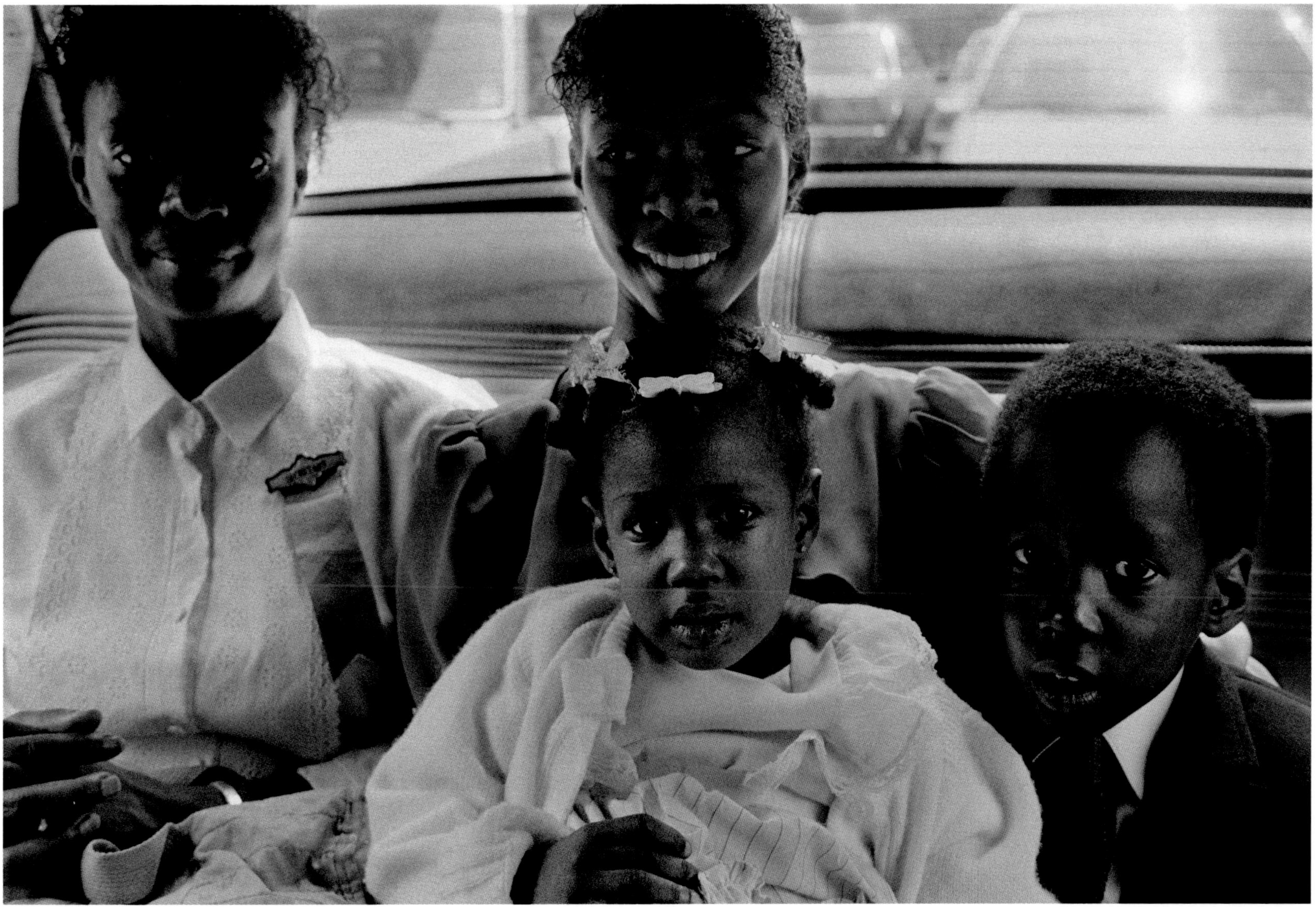

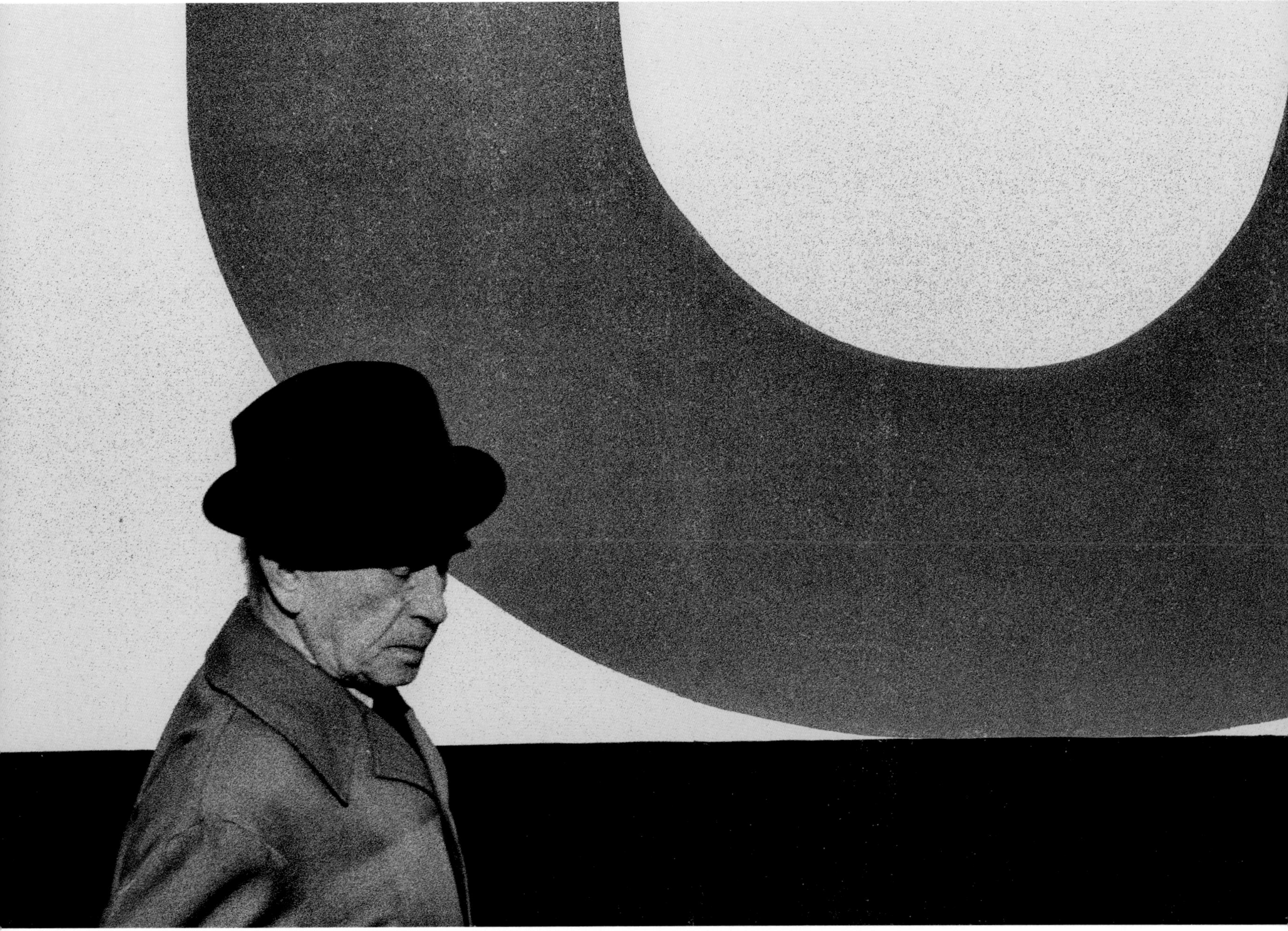

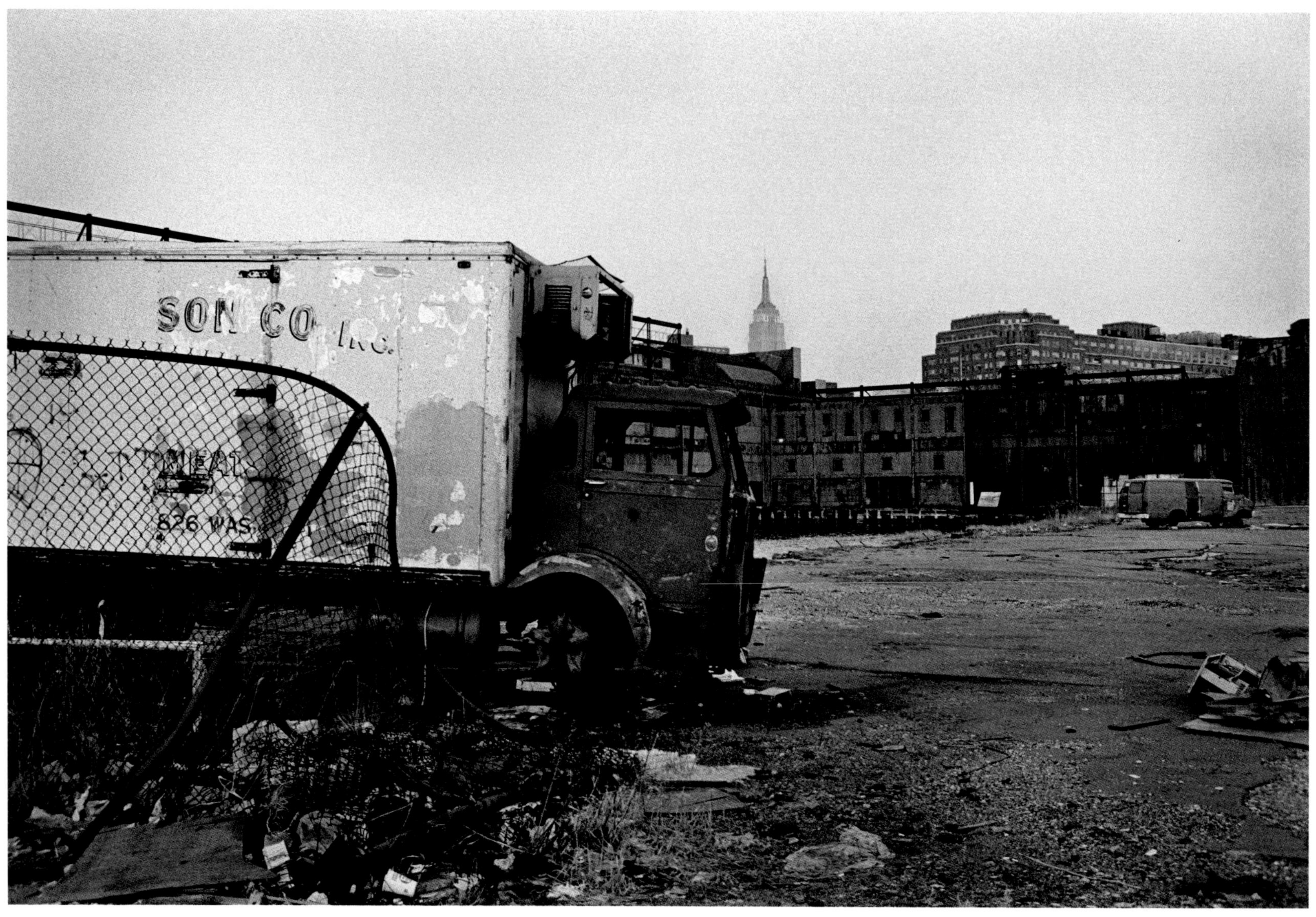
SON CO INC.
826 WAS

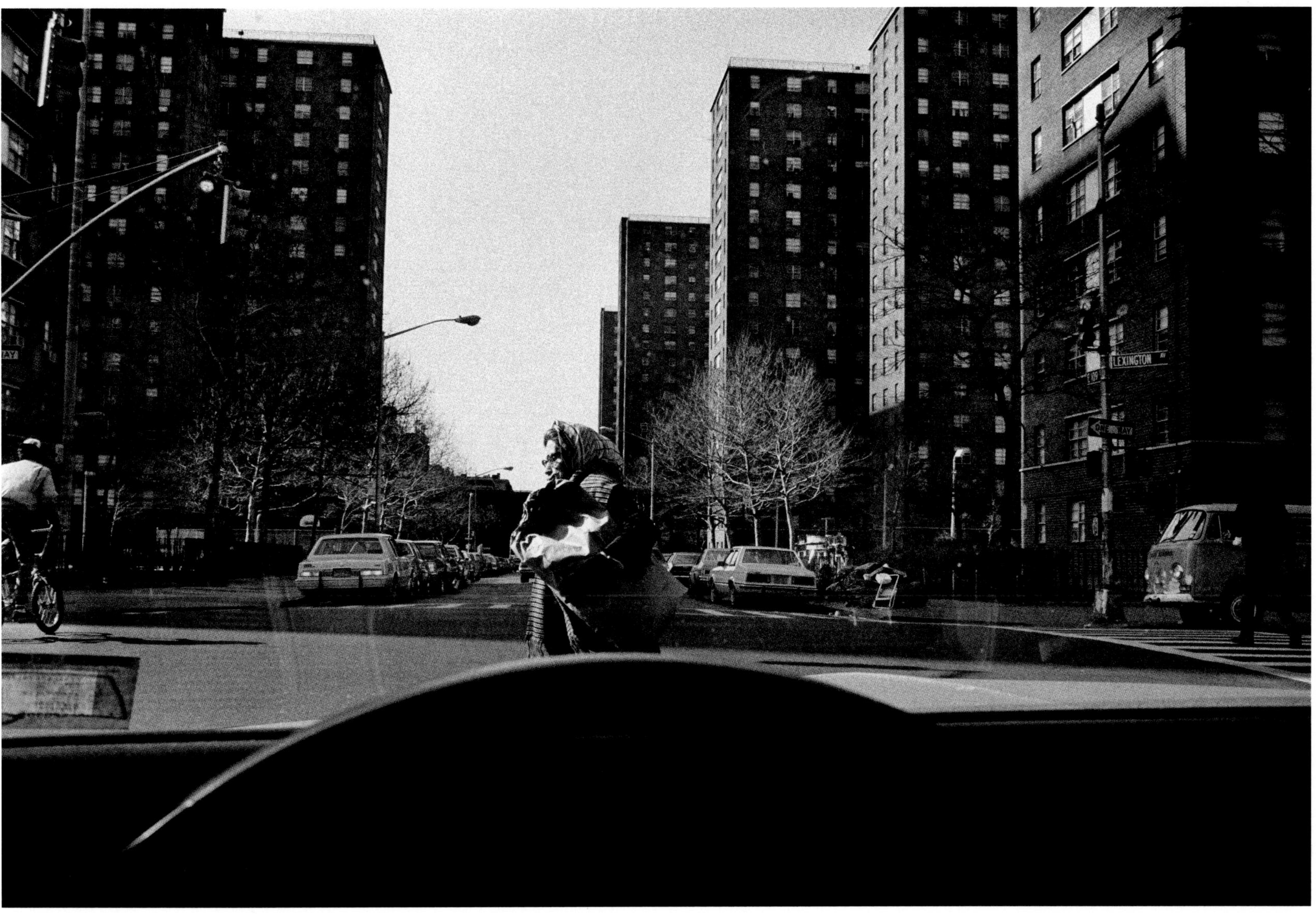
LEXINGTON
ONE WAY

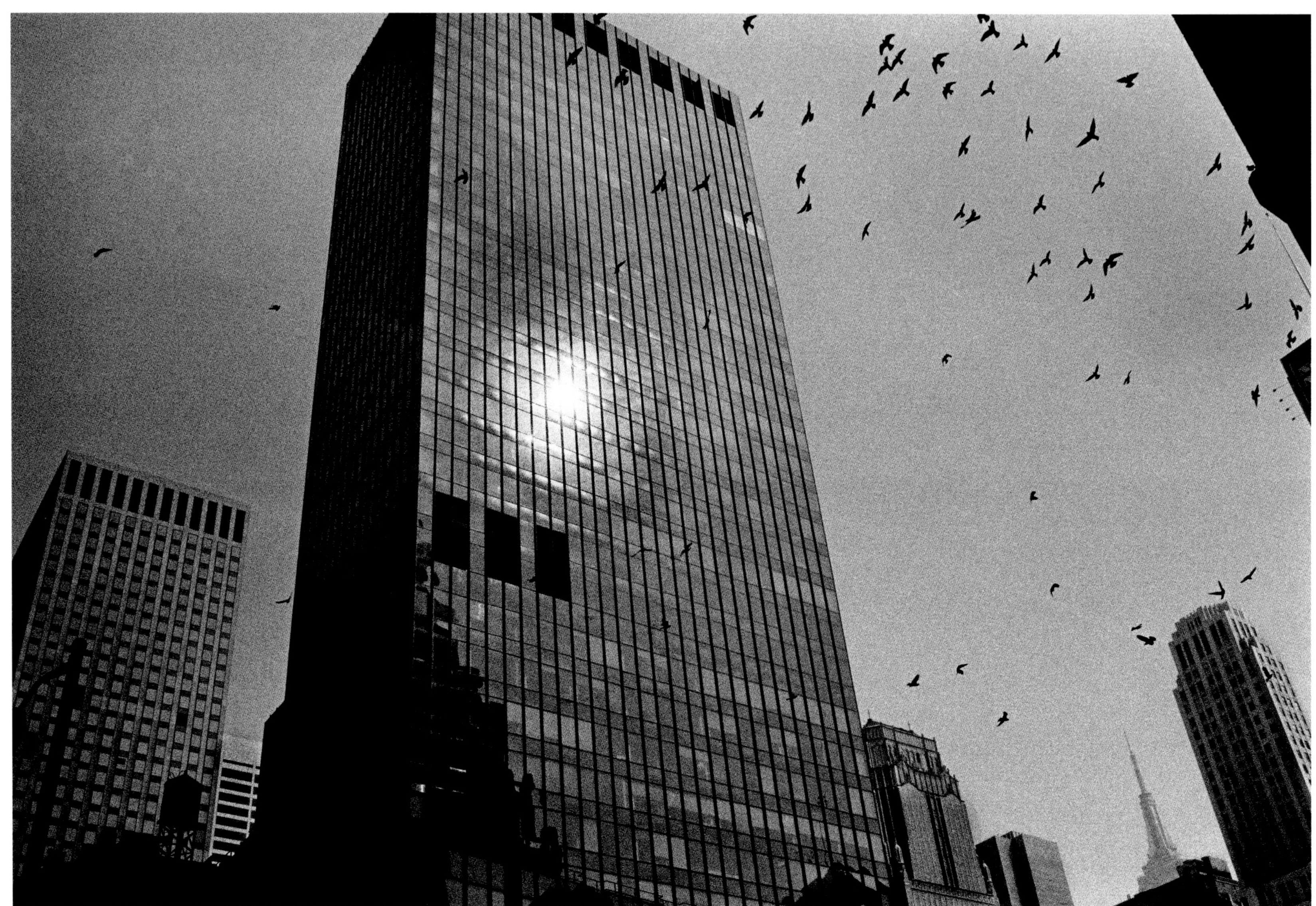

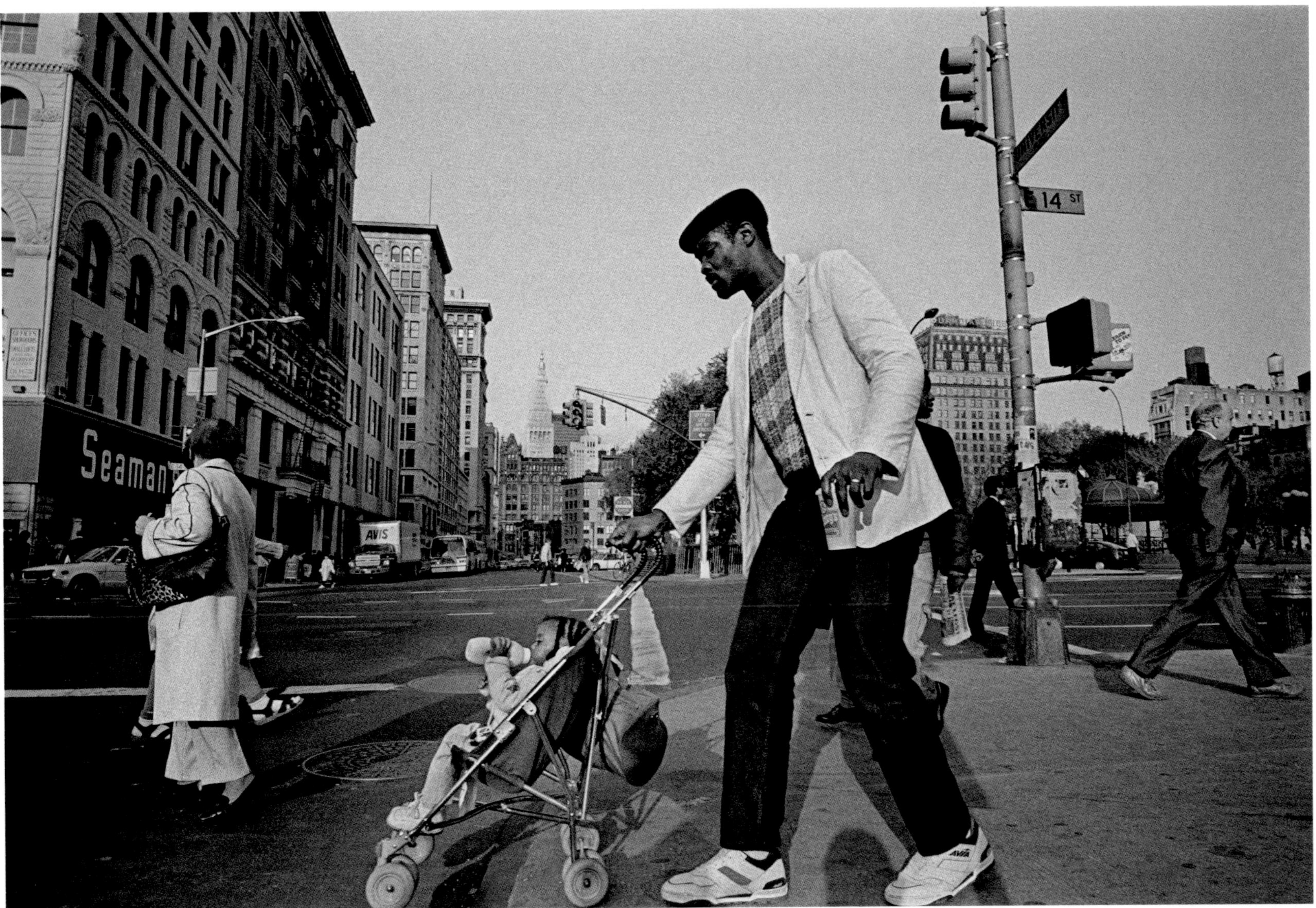
Seaman
AVIS
14 ST
AVIA

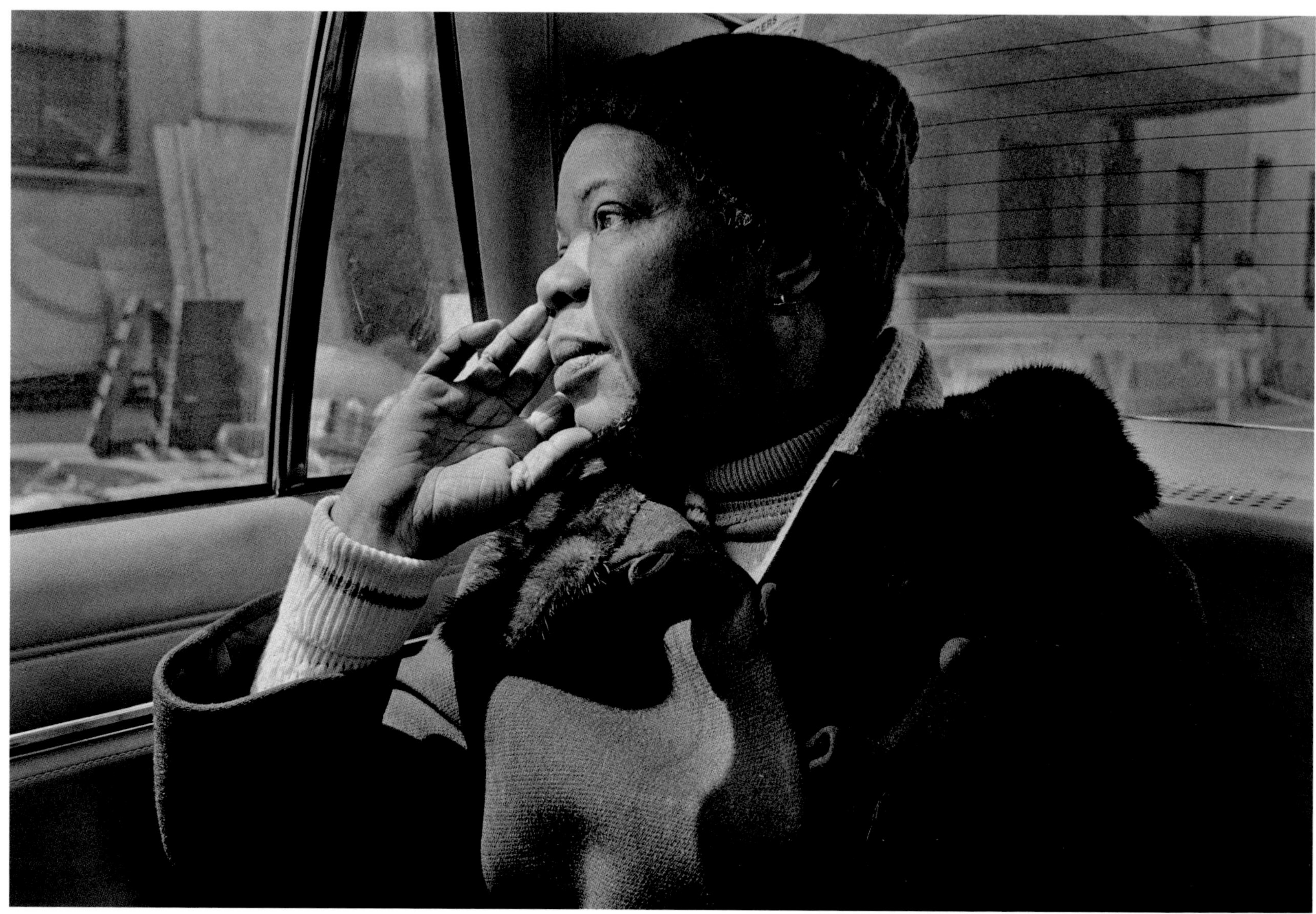

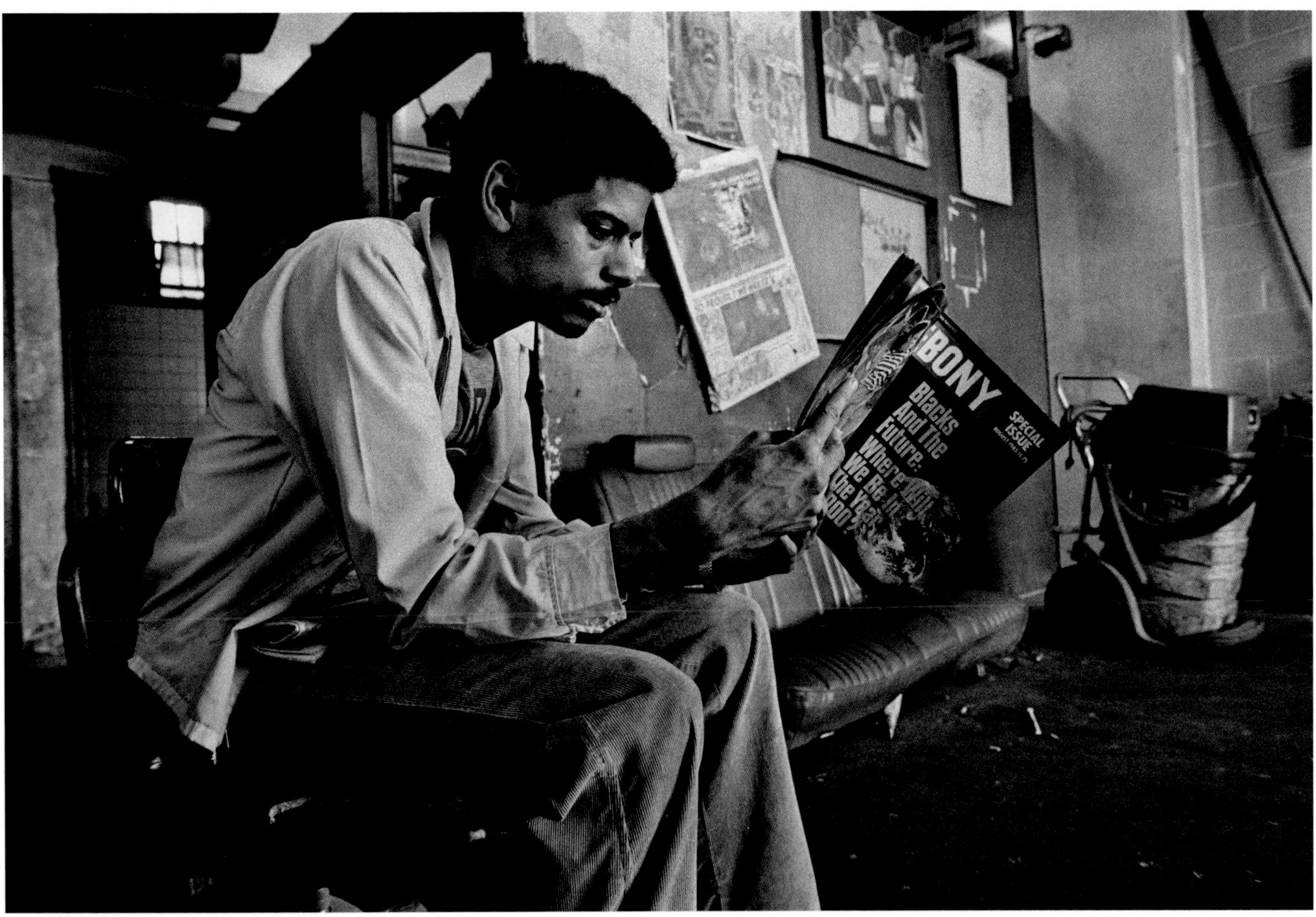
BONY
SPECIAL ISSUE
Blacks
And The
Future:
We Be In

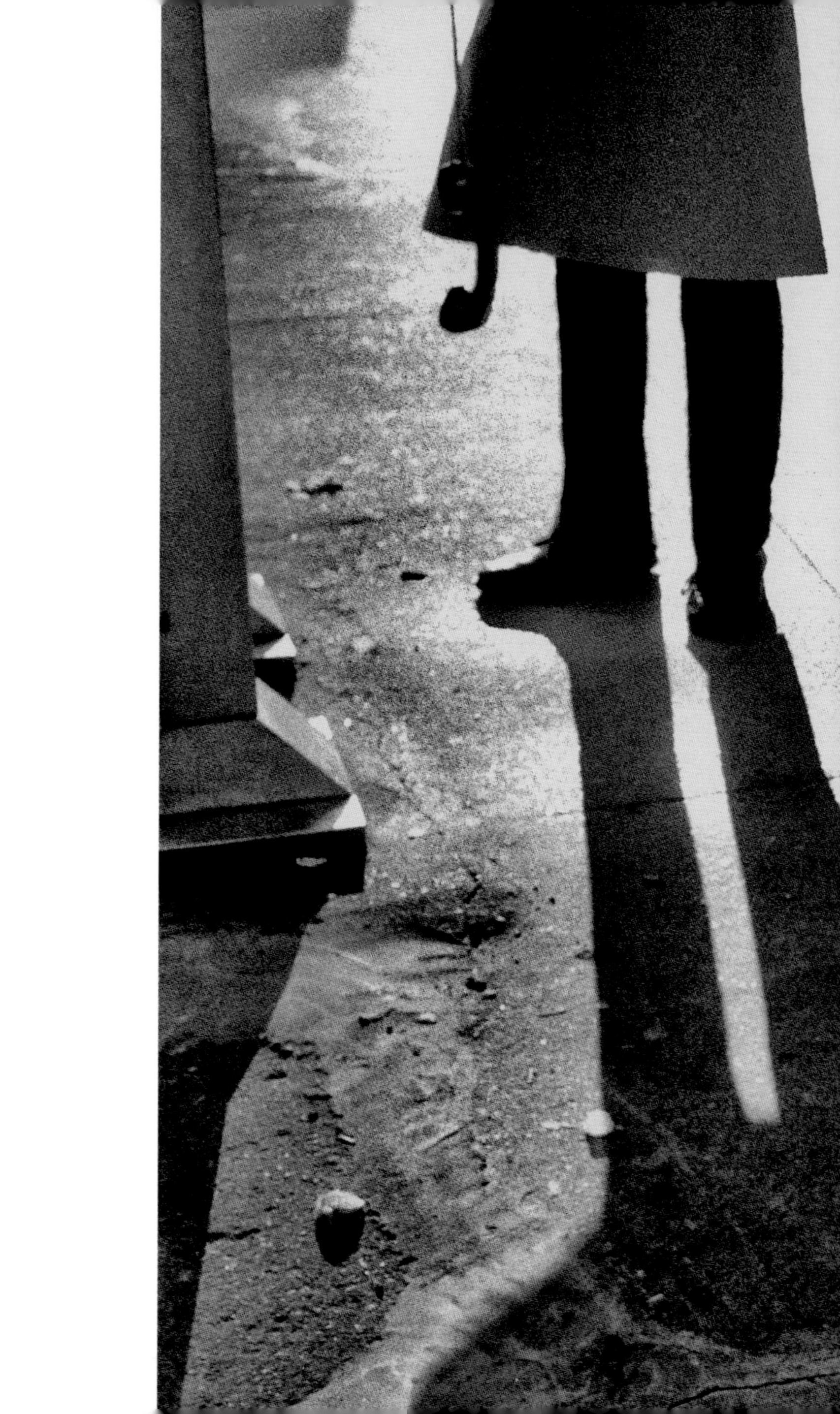

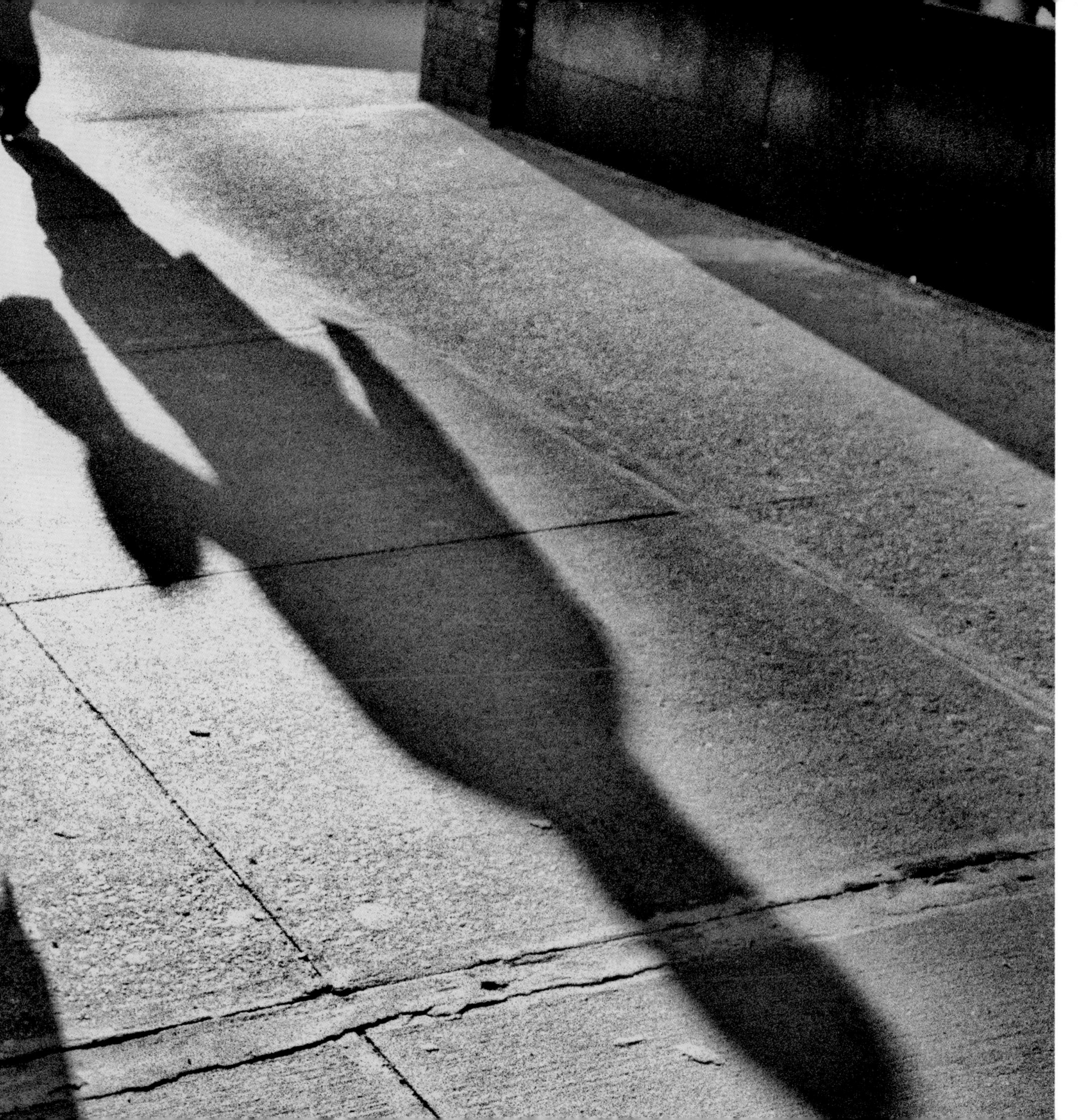

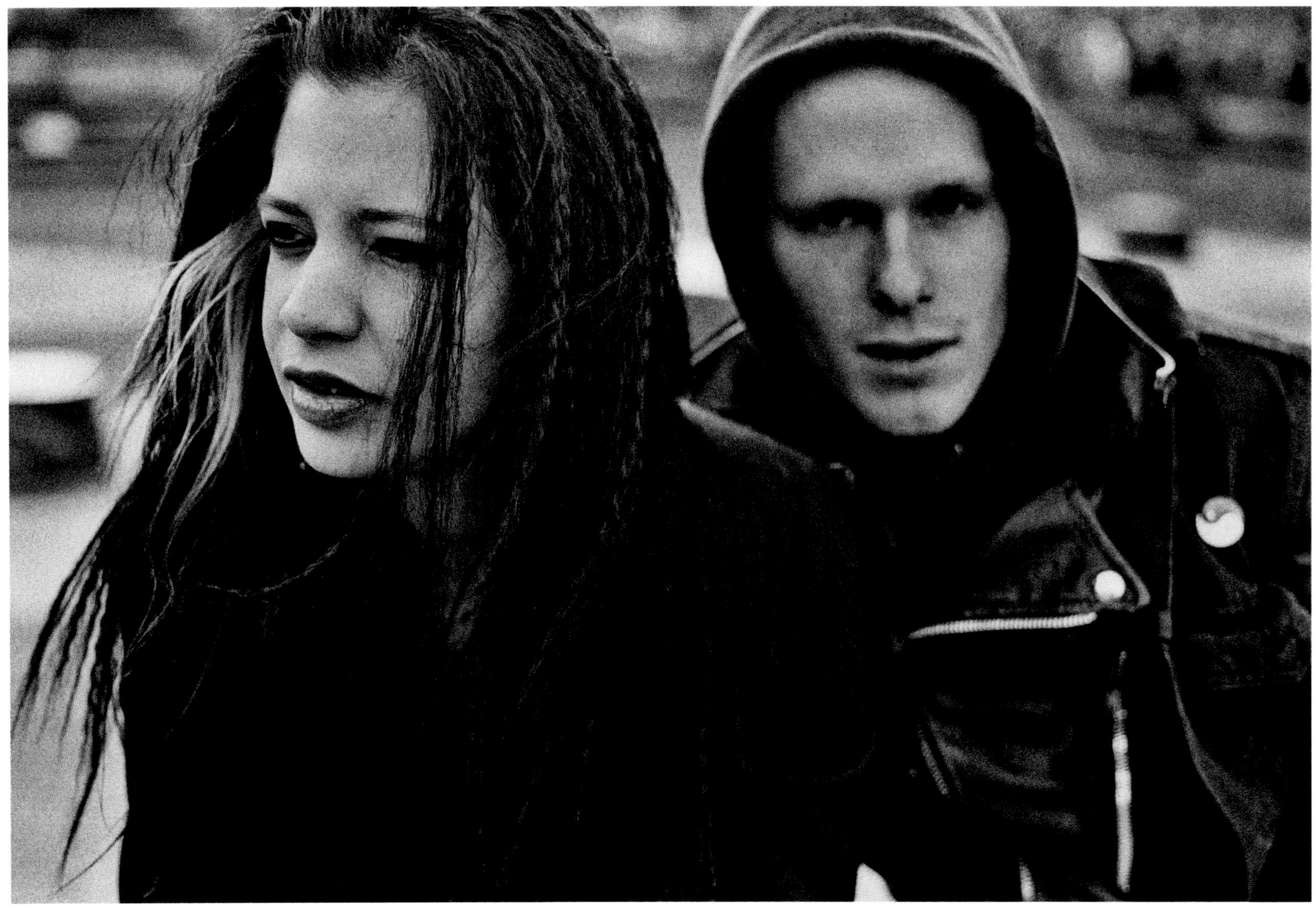

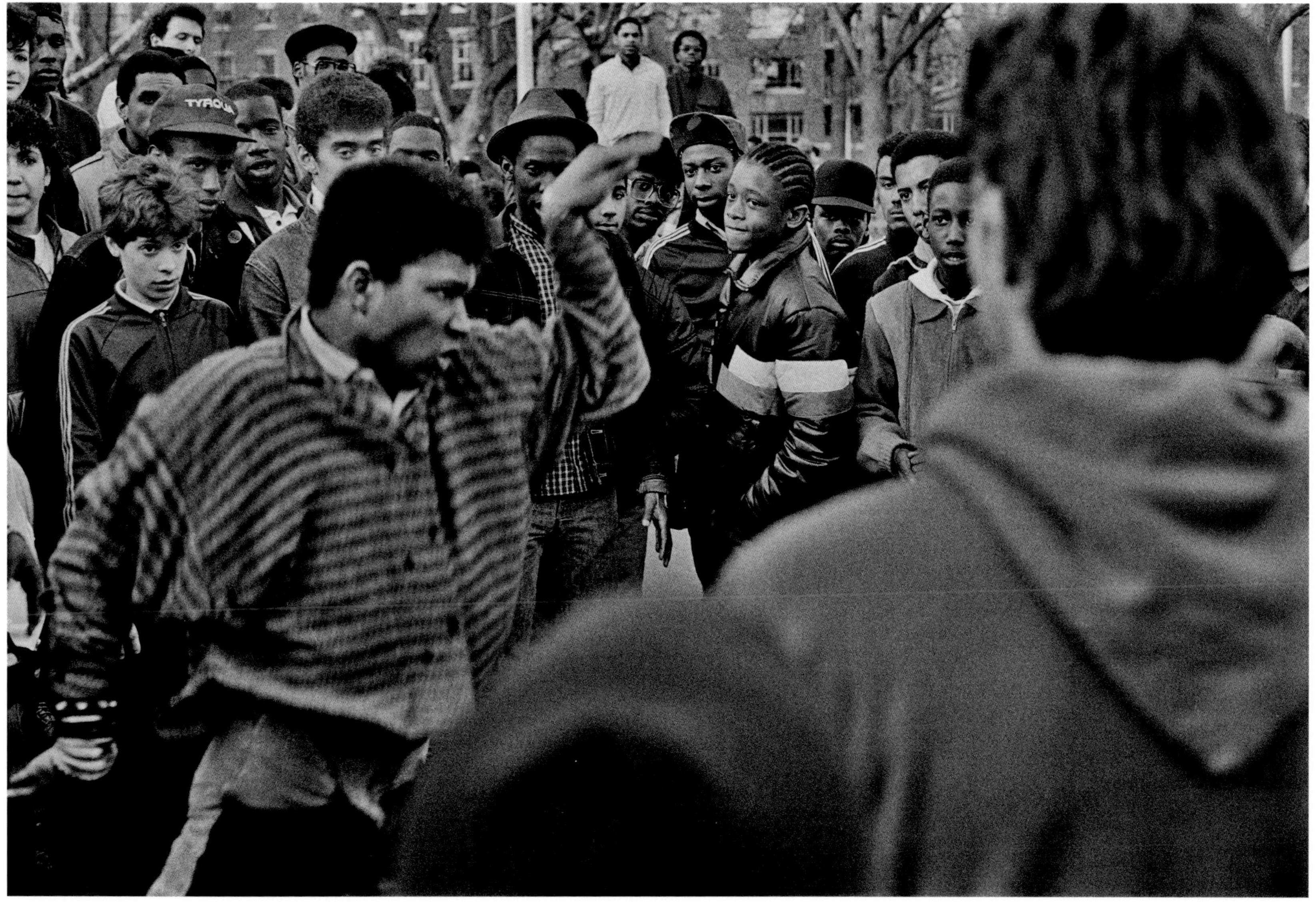

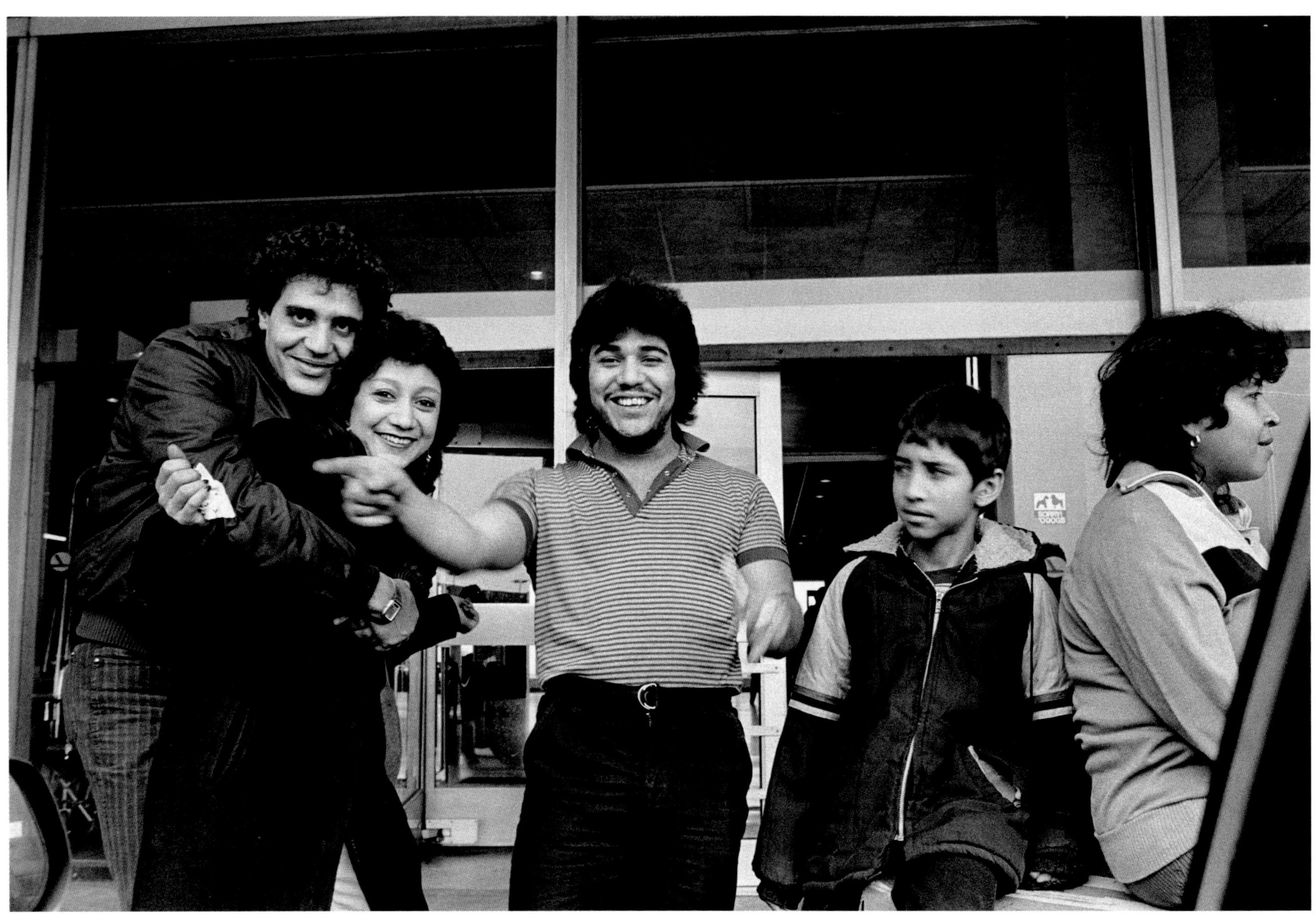

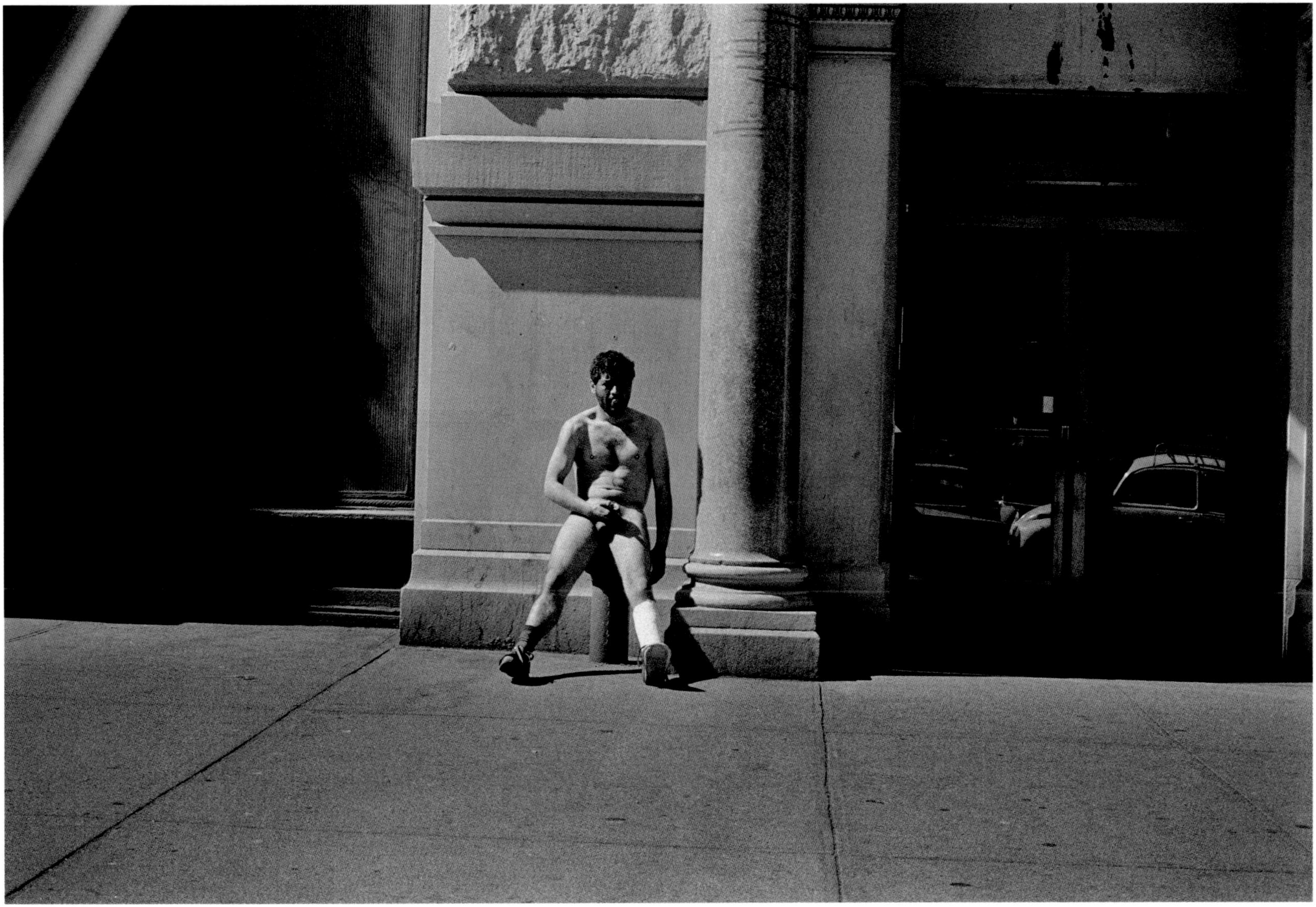

My aunt lived in Stapleton, Staten Island. Back then you could take the car on the ferry. When I got off, the first thing I saw was this guy doing handstands. Then his girlfriend came to him, like so.

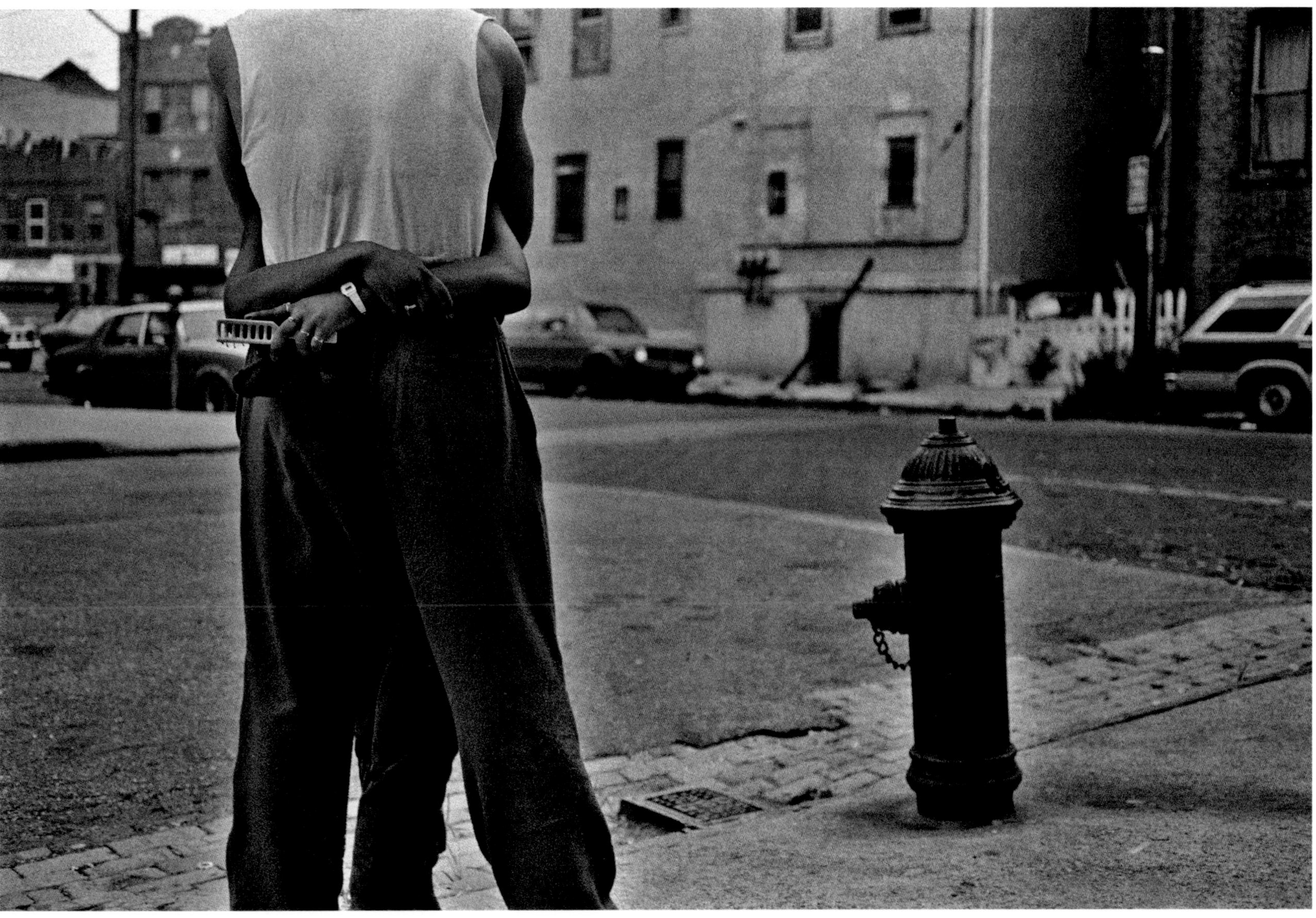

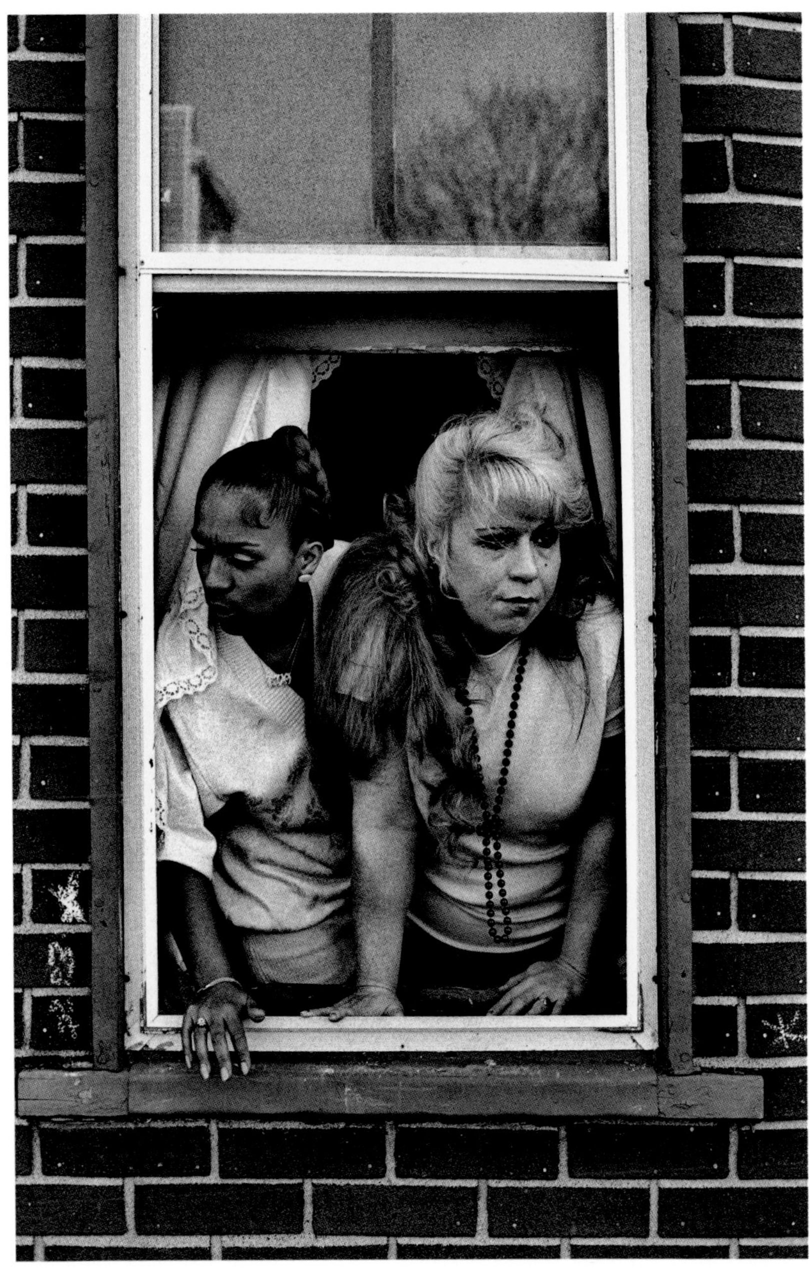

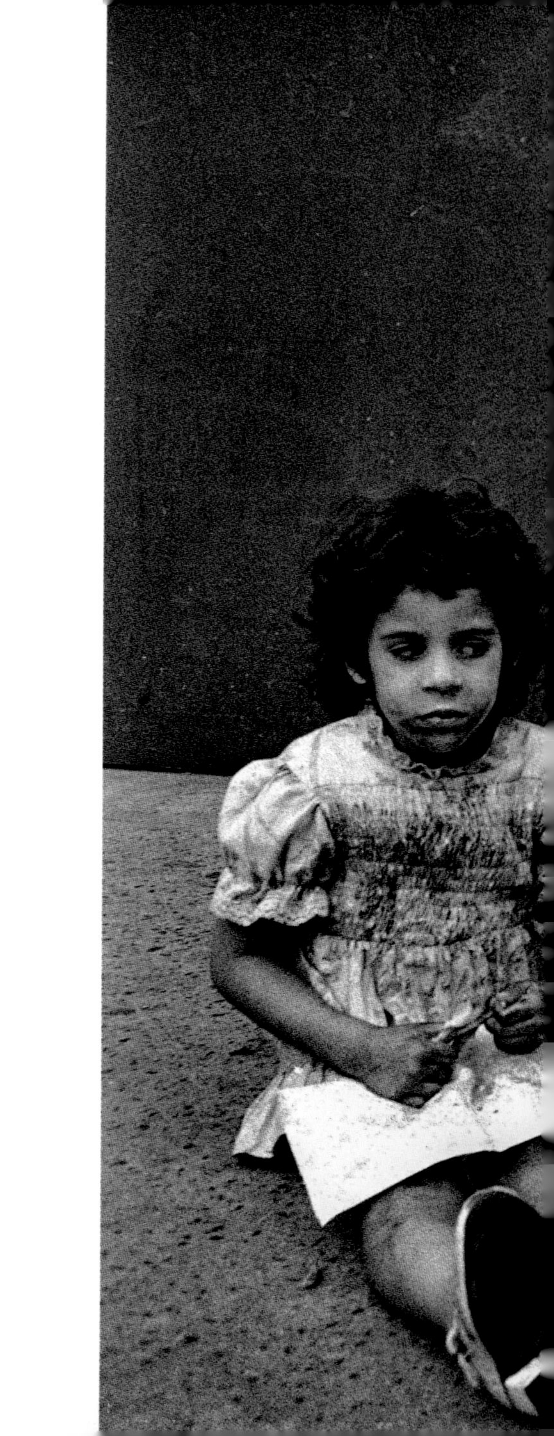

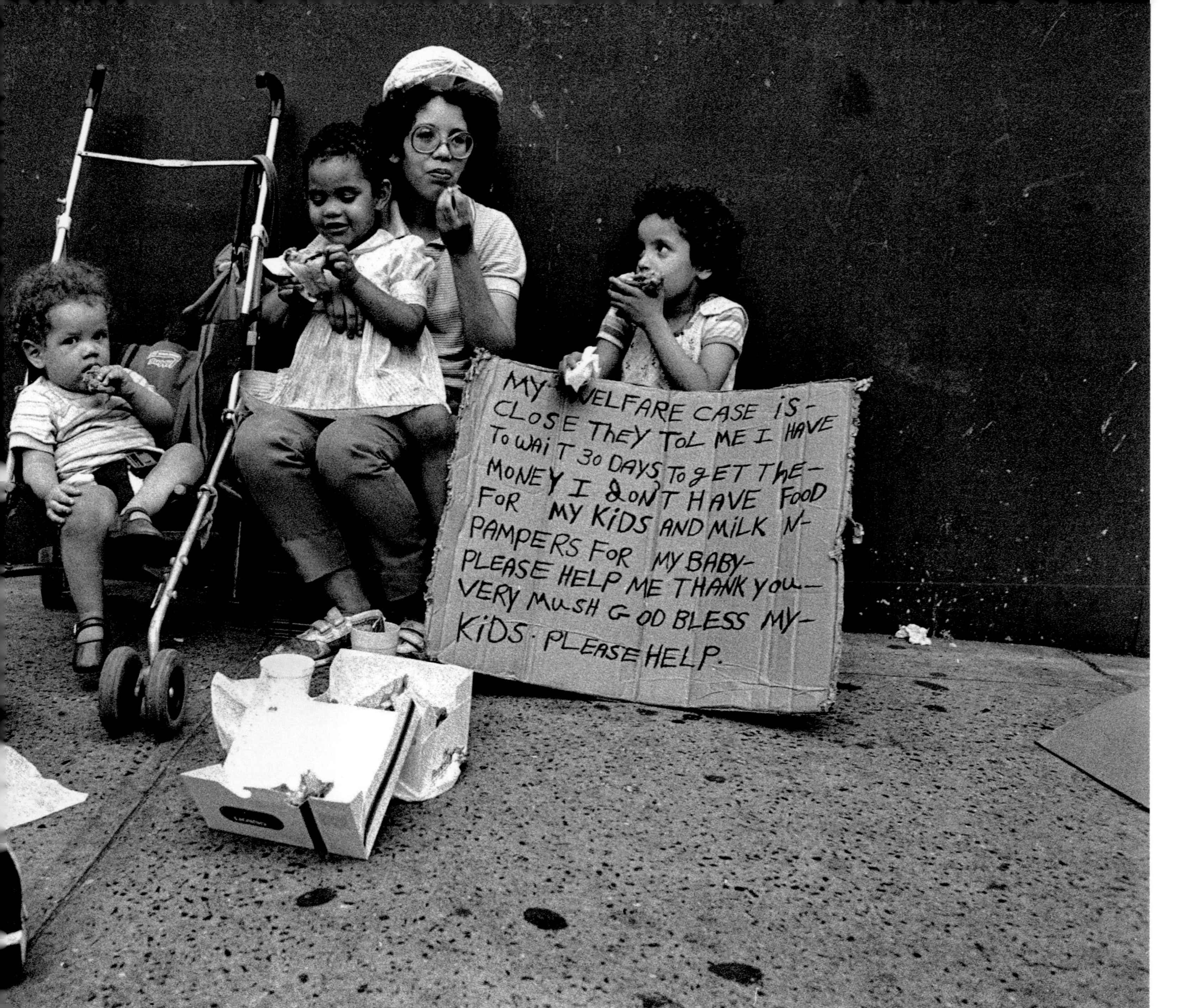
MY WELFARE CASE IS-
CLOSE THEY TOL ME I HAVE
TO WAIT 30 DAYS TO GET THE-
MONEY I DON'T HAVE FOOD
FOR MY KIDS AND MILK N-
PAMPERS FOR MY BABY-
PLEASE HELP ME THANK YOU-
VERY MUSH GOD BLESS MY-
KIDS. PLEASE HELP.

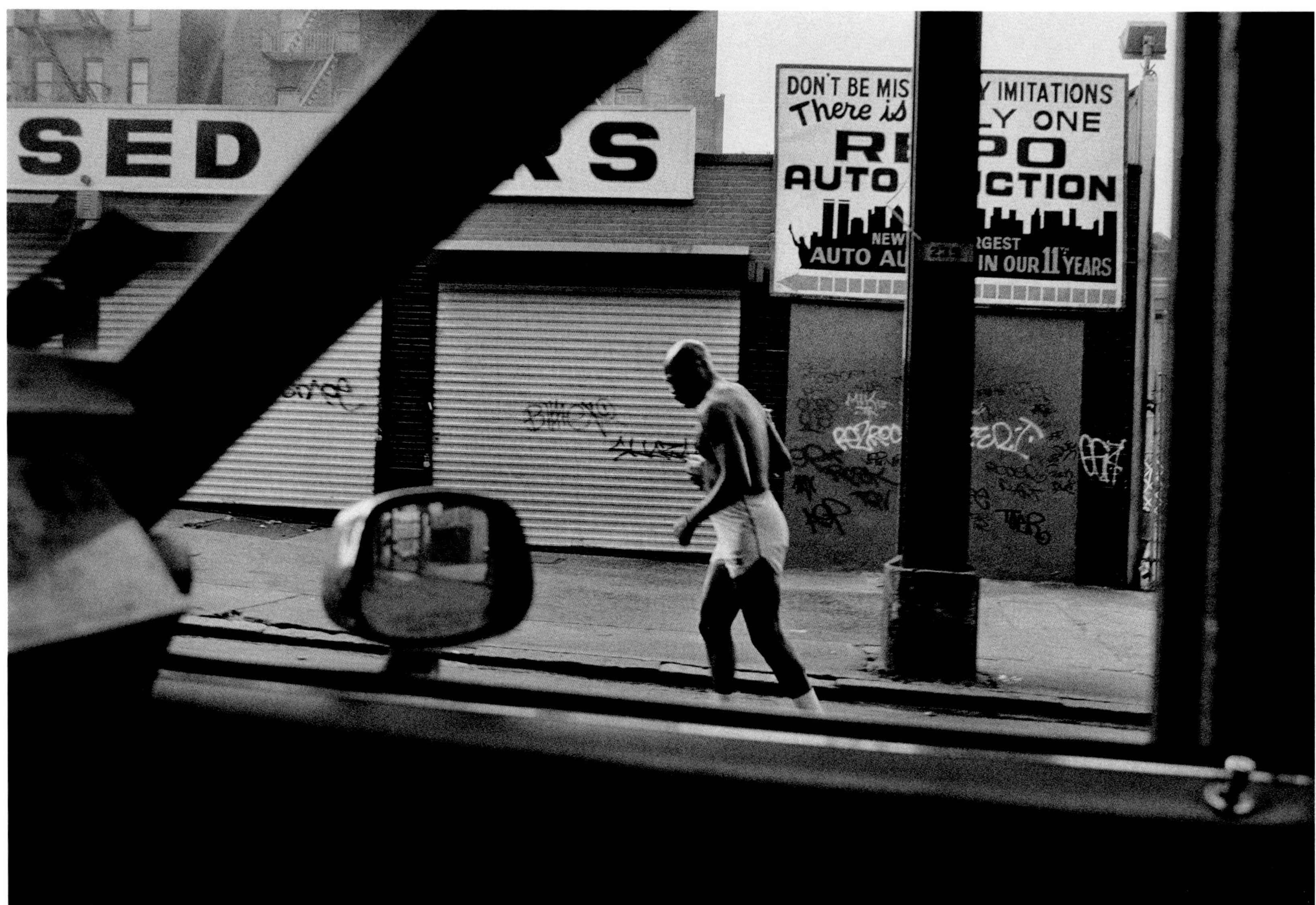
SED
RS
DON'T BE MIS
Y IMITATIONS
There is
LY ONE
AUTO
CTION
NEW
RGEST
AUTO AU
IN OUR 11TH YEARS

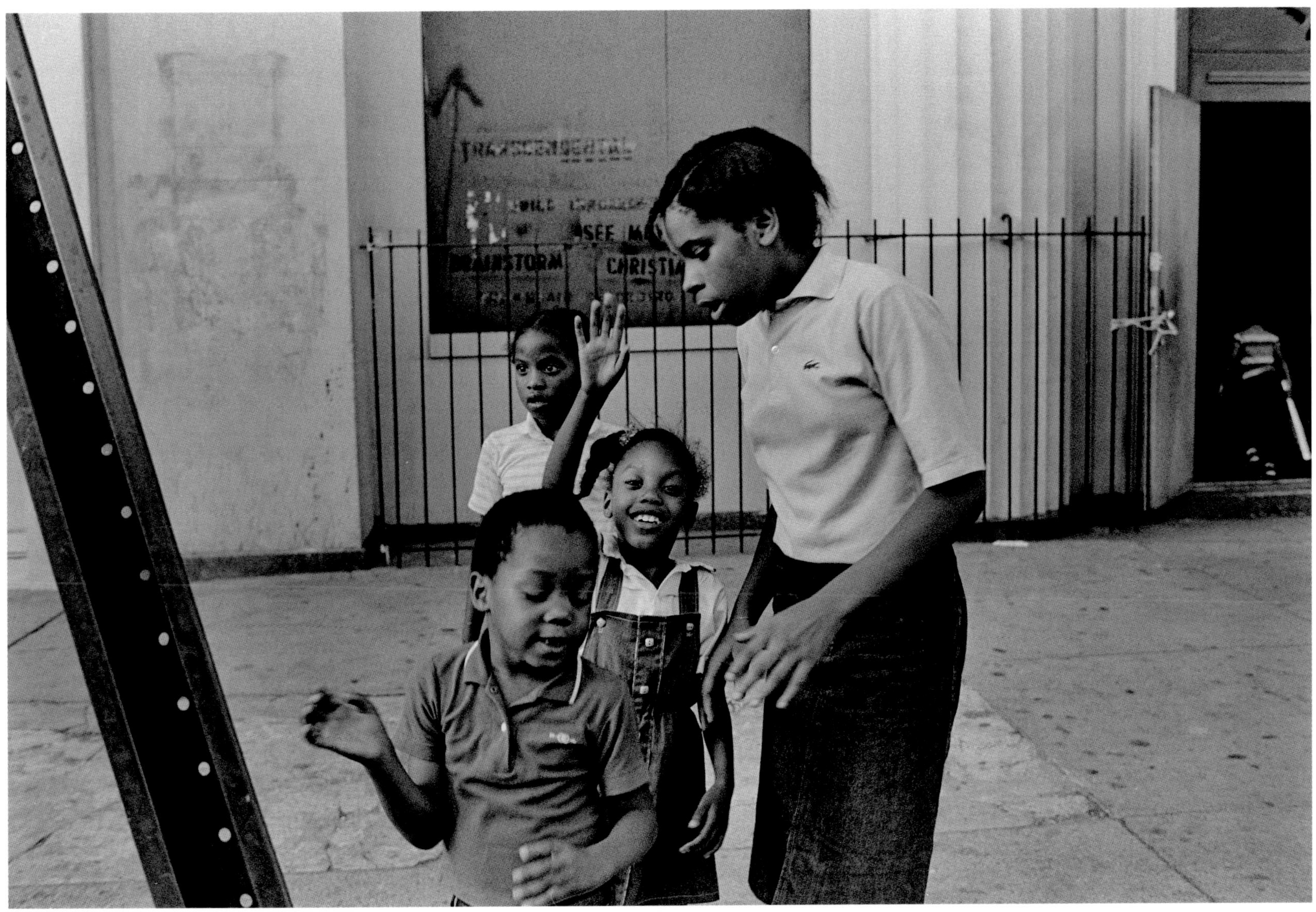
BRAINSTORM

My cab became a hotel room several times. One morning, I was waiting in front of the 220 Club, and this goombah-type guy comes out with a lady of the night and says, "I want to go to Jersey City." "OK," I replied, "it's double the fare." I get the feeling like he might be a mob-connected guy—he's got that tone. We get out to Jersey City, and we stop at a diner, and he says, "OK, I want to use your cab." So I go into the diner and have my breakfast, and I assume they're having sex in the back seat. When I come out, he gives me the money and I go back into the city empty. Another time, picked up two guys Downtown, and I was coming across the Central Park transverse at 65th Street, from west to east. I stopped at the light at Fifth Avenue, right across from Temple Emanu-El, the biggest synagogue in Manhattan. All of a sudden, everybody's staring at my cab. I'm like, "What the fuck is going on?" but I have a cab with one of those plastic shields, and I can't really see into the back seat too well. I turn around and look through the shield, and one guy is performing oral sex on the other. I pull over on Fifth and yell at them to get out of my cab. You know why? 'Cause they didn't even ask.

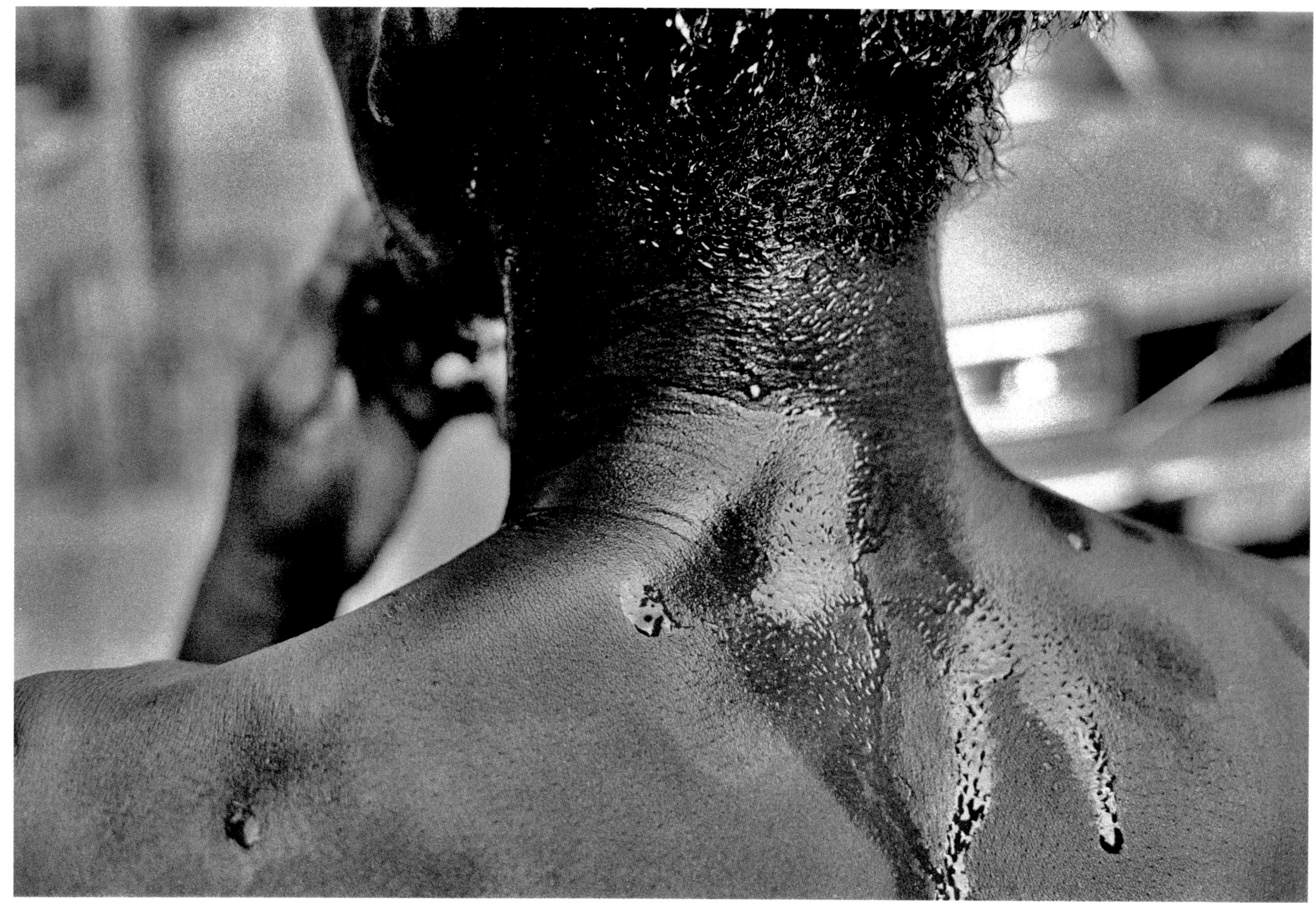

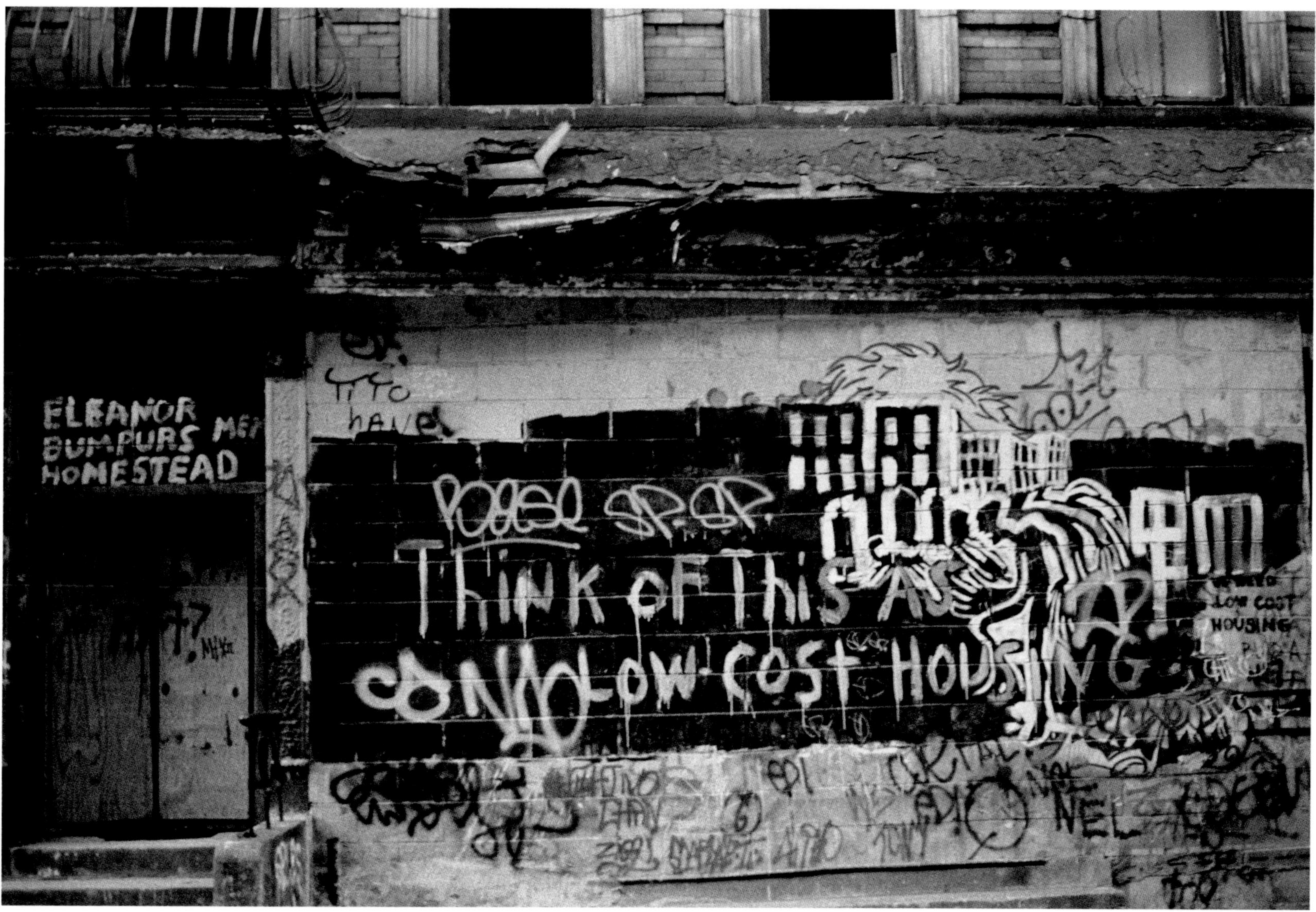
ELEANOR
BUMPURS
HOMESTEAD
THINK OF THIS AS
LOW·COST HOUSING
LOW COST
HOUSING

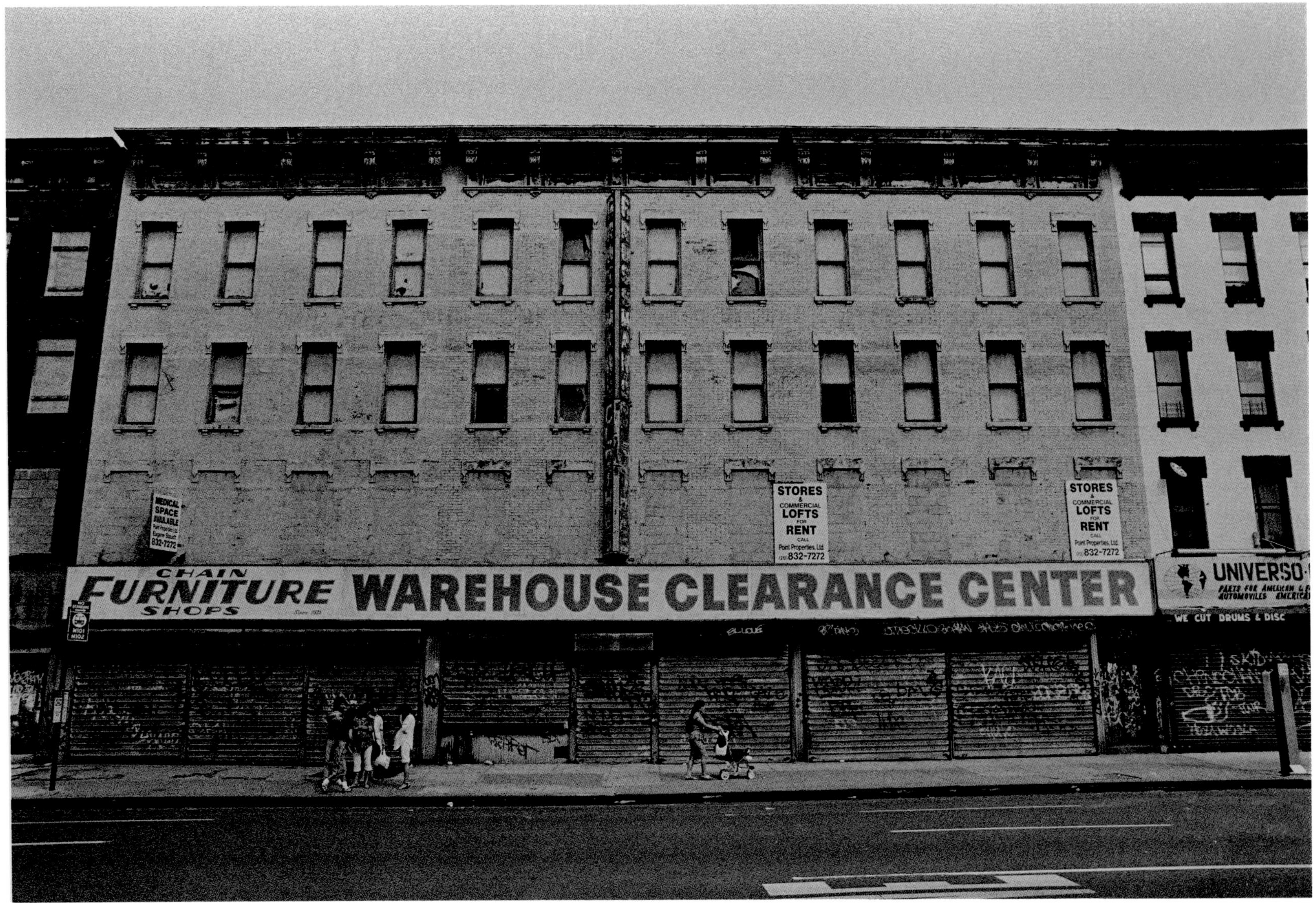
CHAIN
FURNITURE
SHOPS
WAREHOUSE CLEARANCE CENTER
STORES
COMMERCIAL
LOFTS
FOR
RENT
CALL
Point Properties, Ltd
832-7272
STORES
COMMERCIAL
LOFTS
FOR
RENT
CALL
Point Properties, Ltd
832-7272
MEDICAL
SPACE
AVAILABLE
832-7272
UNIVERSO
WE CUT DRUMS & DISC

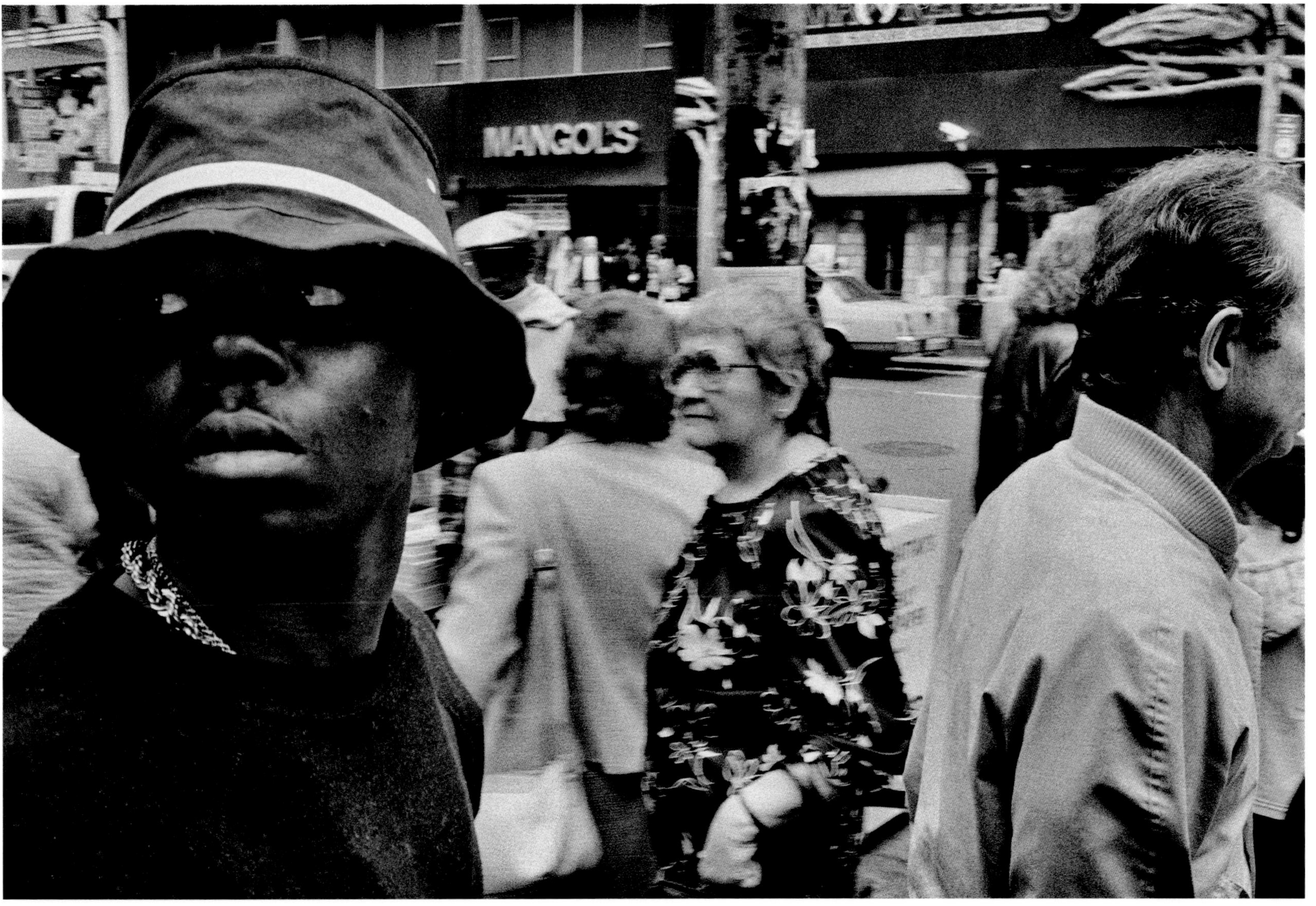
MANGOL'S

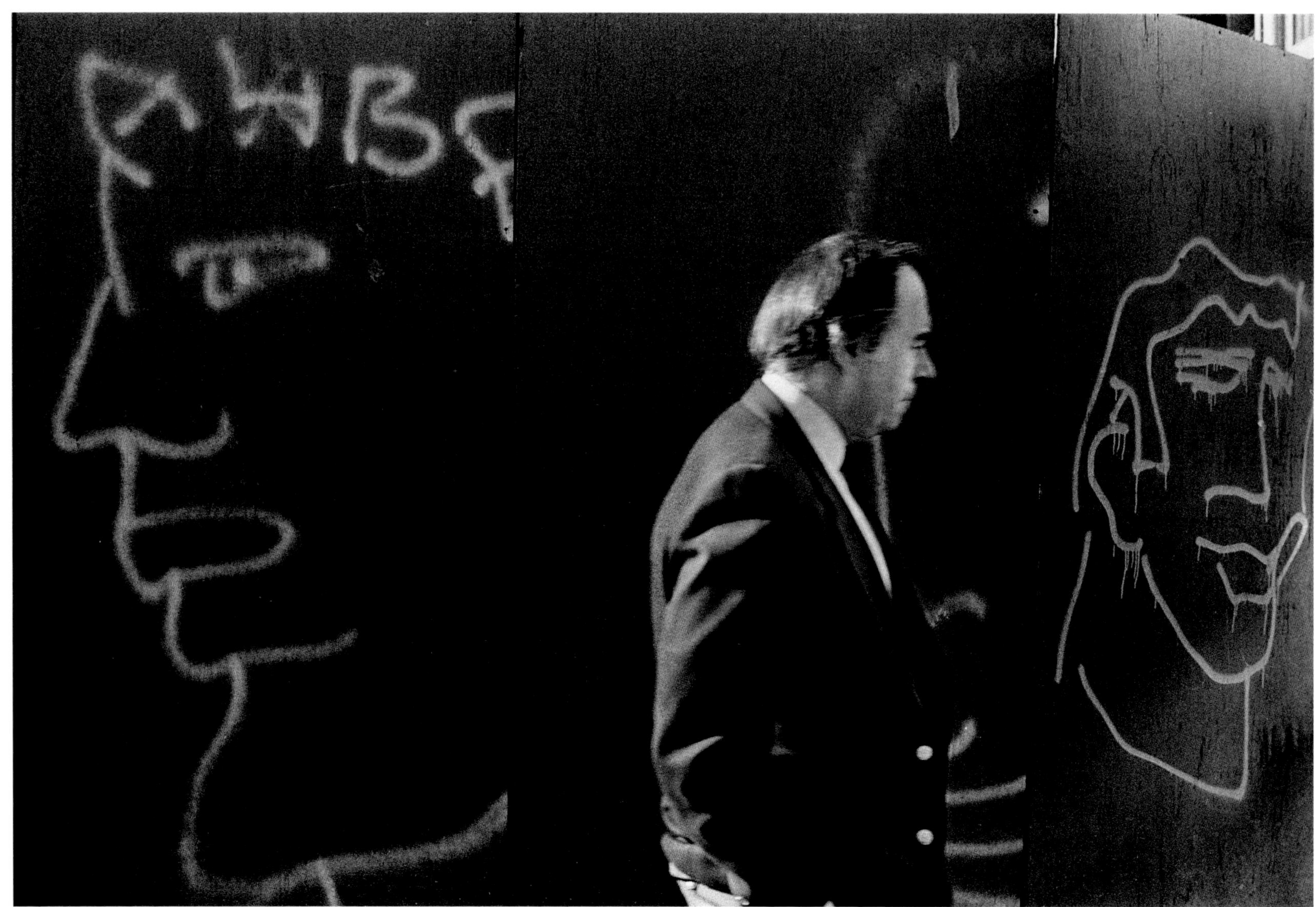

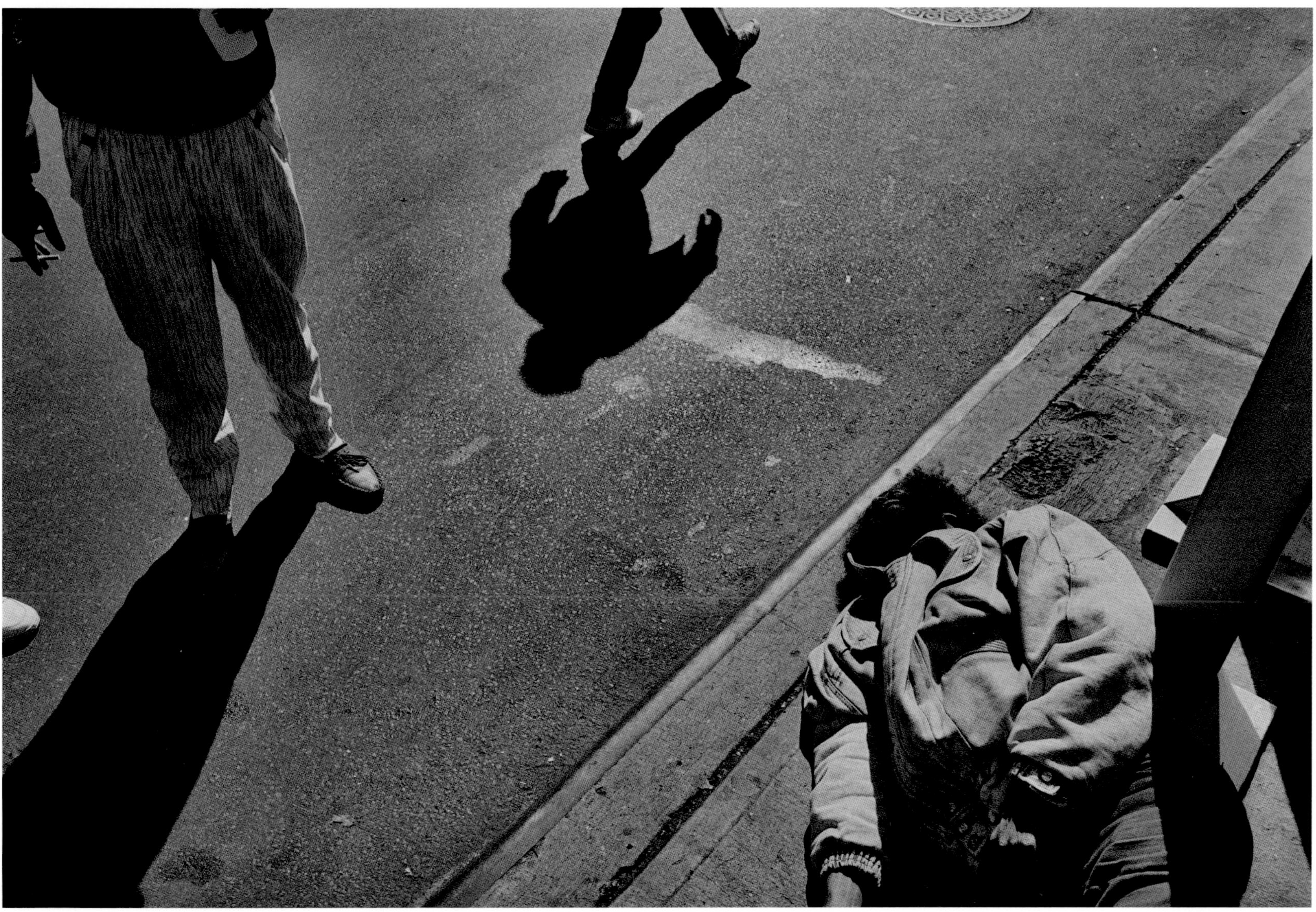

At the beginning of the shift, I didn't have to go far. I'd pull out onto 15th Street at four-thirty in the morning, and there was a line of sex workers standing on just about every corner.

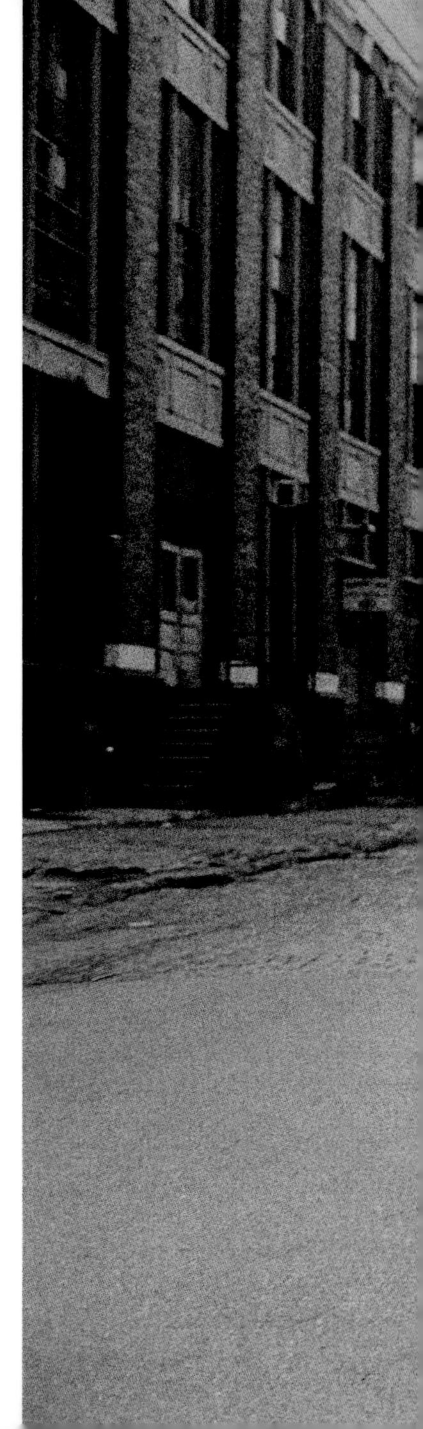

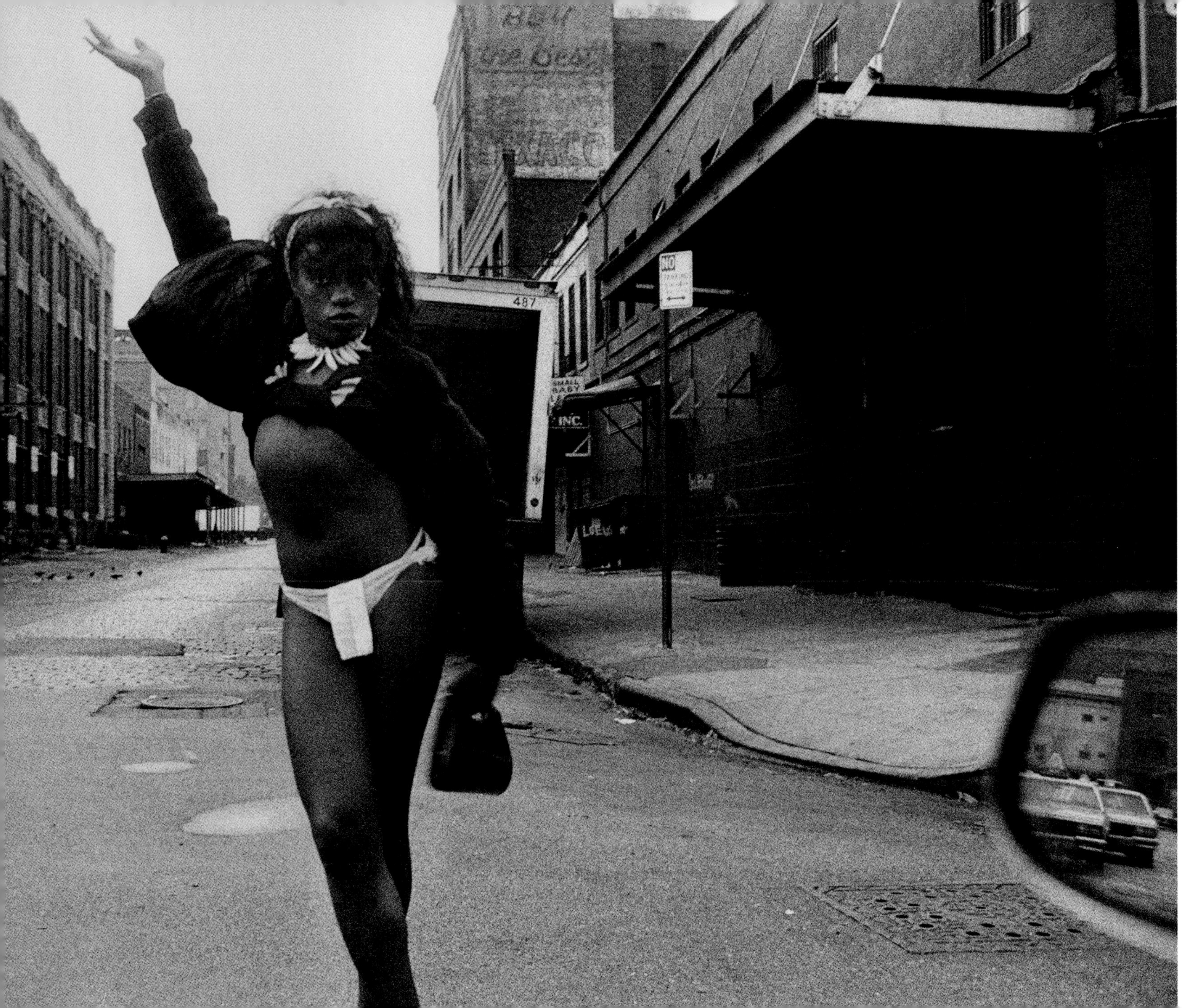
487
NO
INC.

A CAB BECOMES a place to hear stories.
It also becomes like a pyschiatrist's office.
People have so much to tell you.

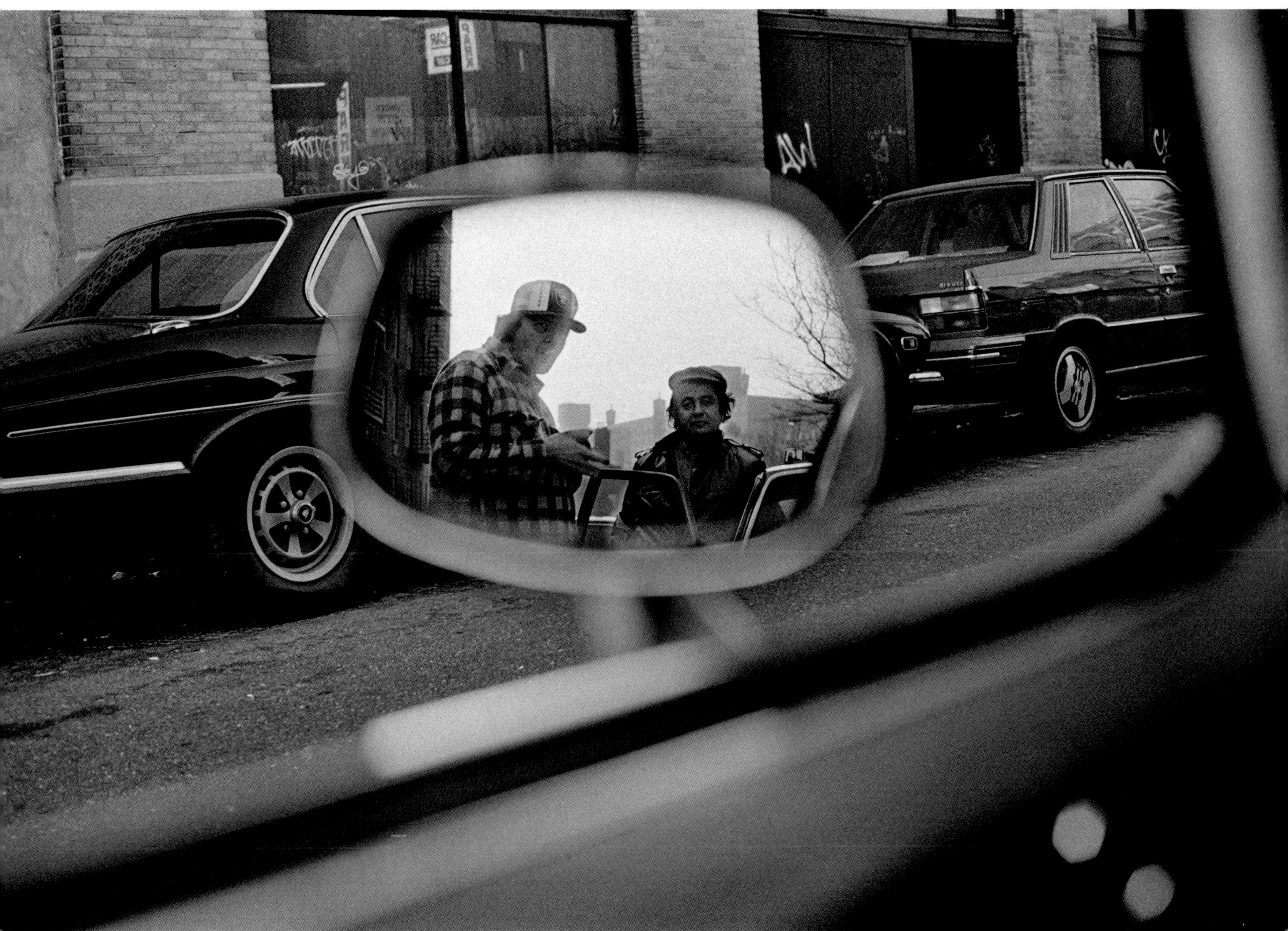

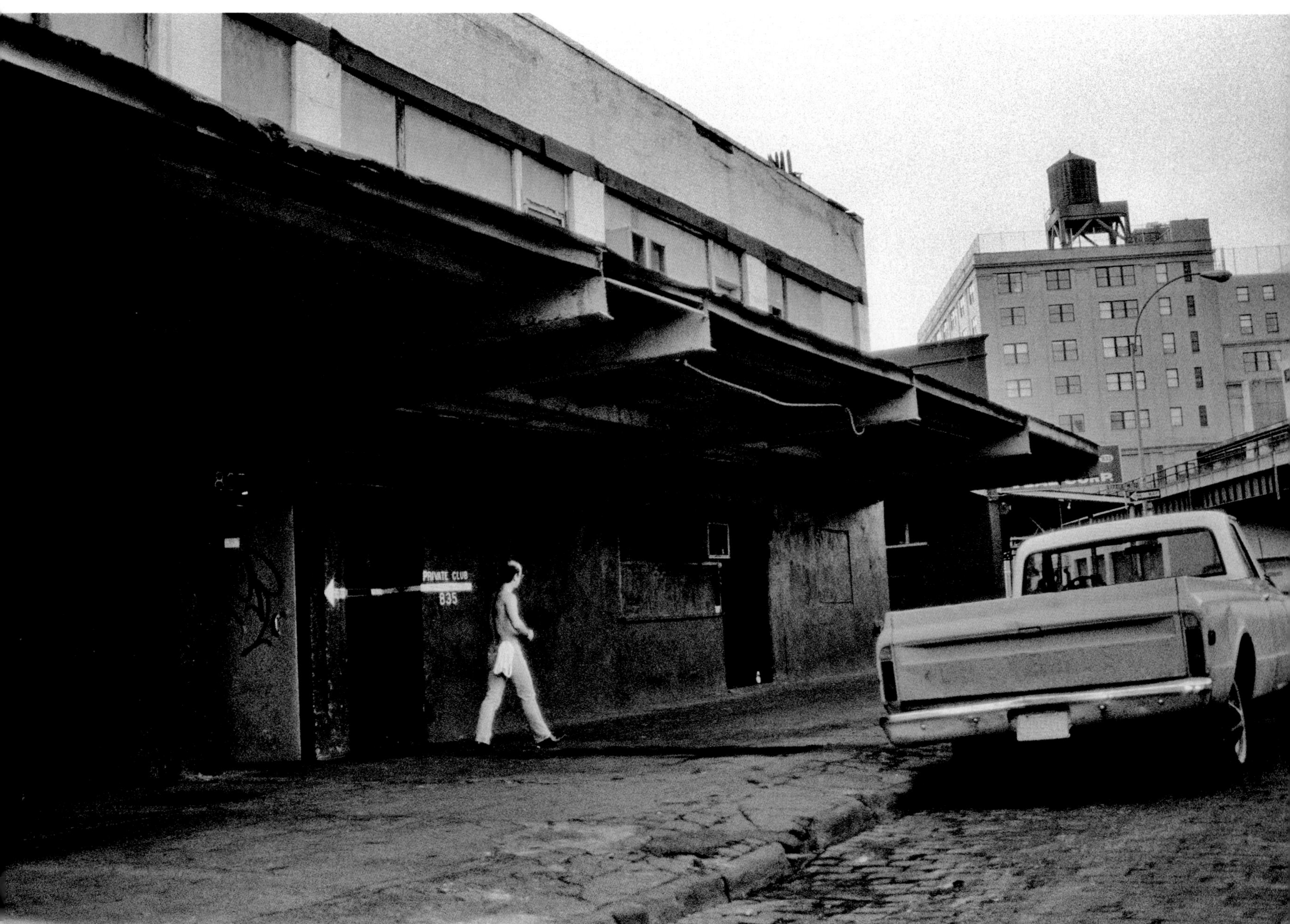
PRIVATE CLUB
835

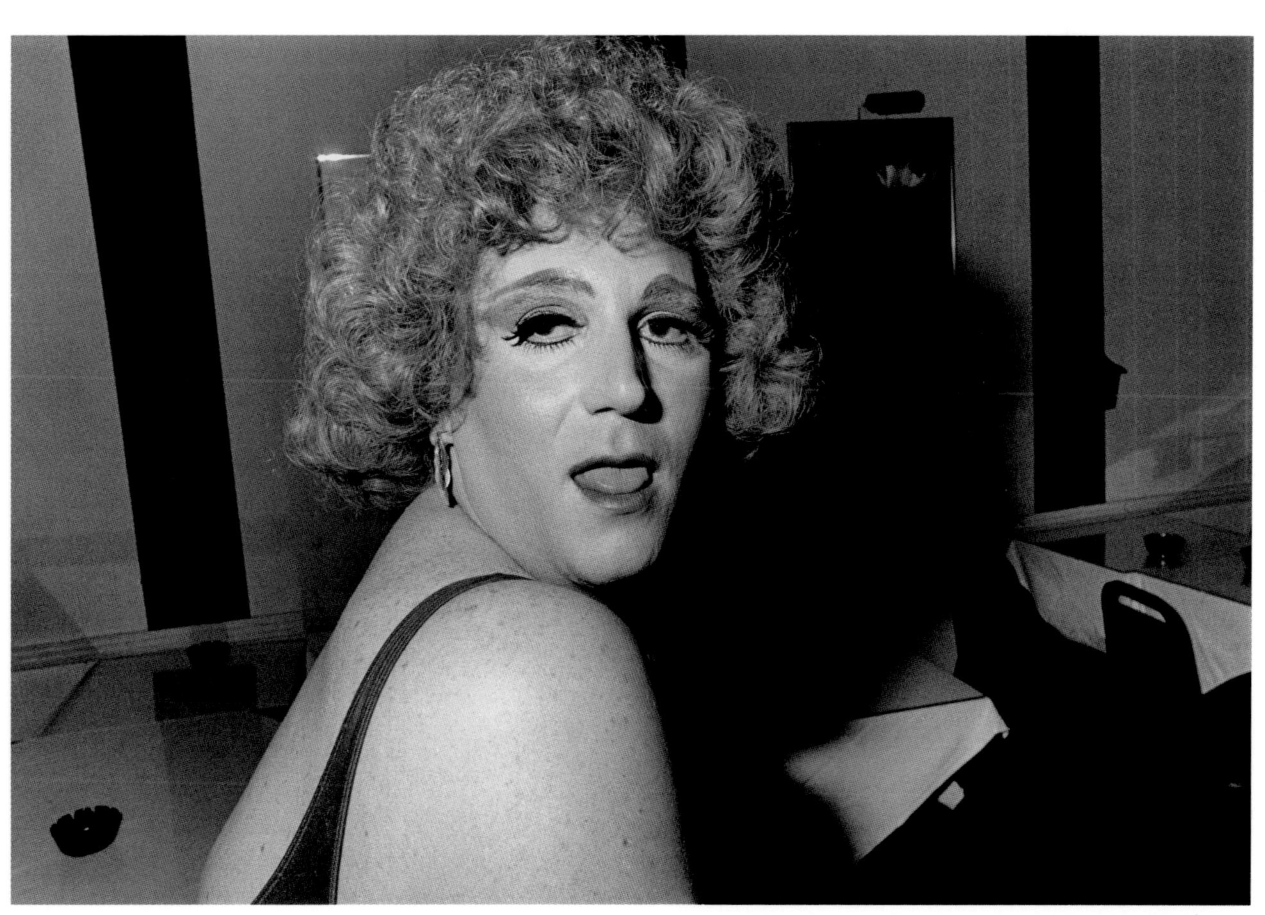

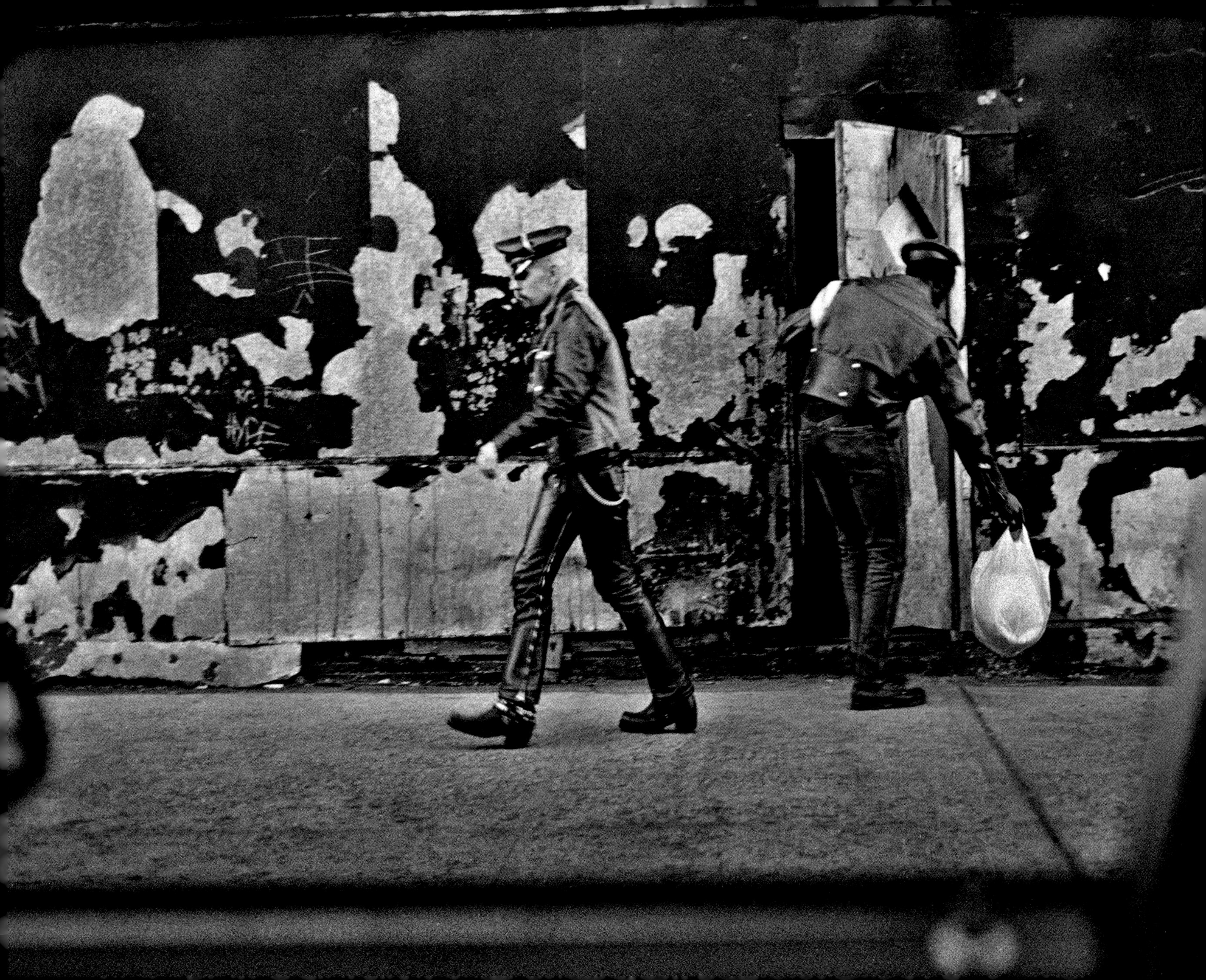

I USED TO WORK THE S&M CLUBS because those were the long fares. There was one fare I picked up at the Hellfire on Washington Street—leather chaps, ass-out, leather hat. By the time we got to 89TH Street, he was wearing a pink oxford shirt and penny loafers. "Good morning, sir," the doorman said.

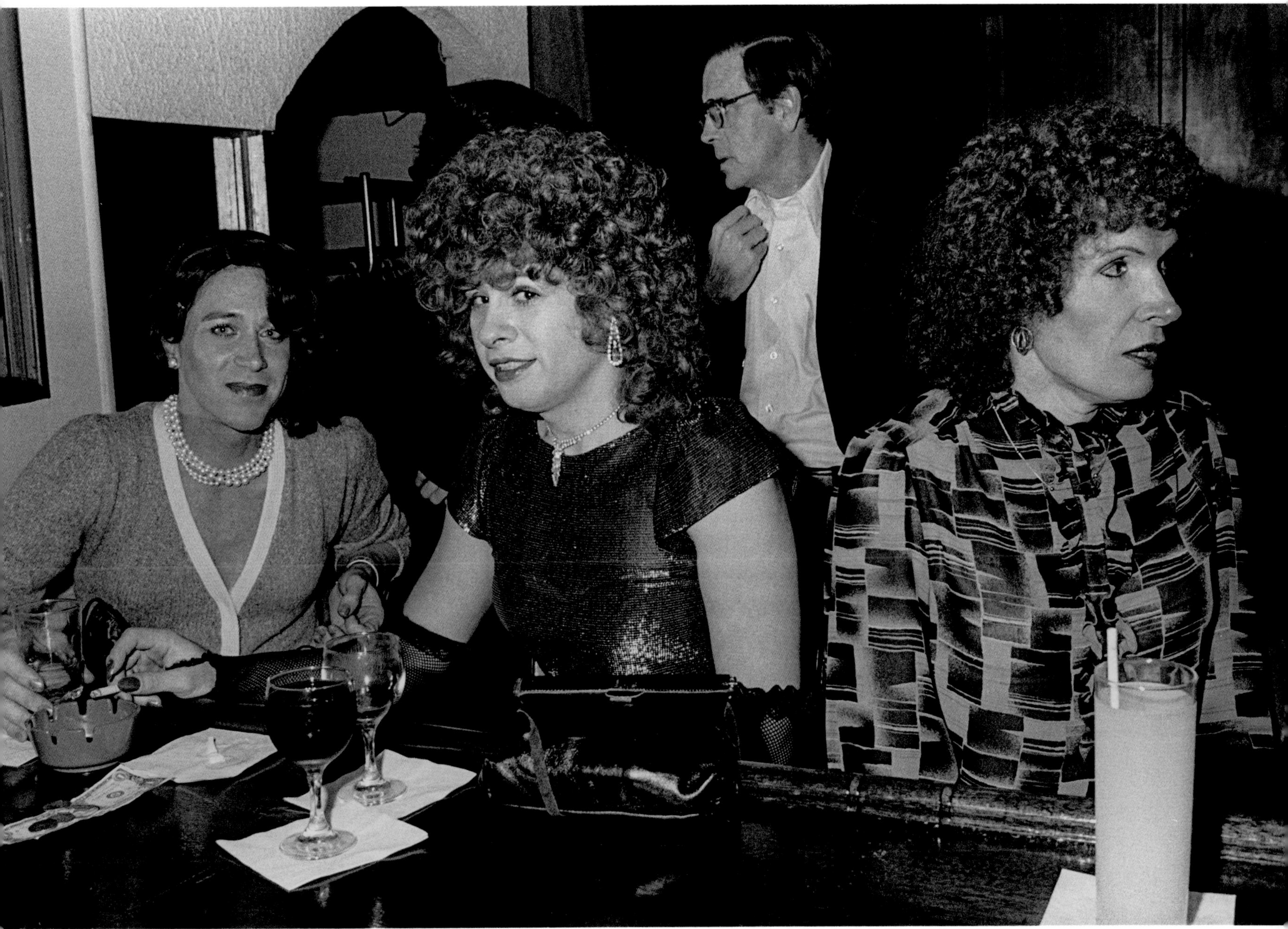

THE MEATPACKING DISTRICT was literally that. There were no fancy shoe stores. It smelled like meat, it felt like meat, it was meat. It was like a living metaphor. I would pick up these guys—lonely…sad…depressed… dark… Most of the time, it didn't seem like they were searching for love—it seemed like they were searching for sex. The Hideaway Hotel was upstairs from the Anvil. Guys would meet somebody at the Anvil, and go right up to a room.

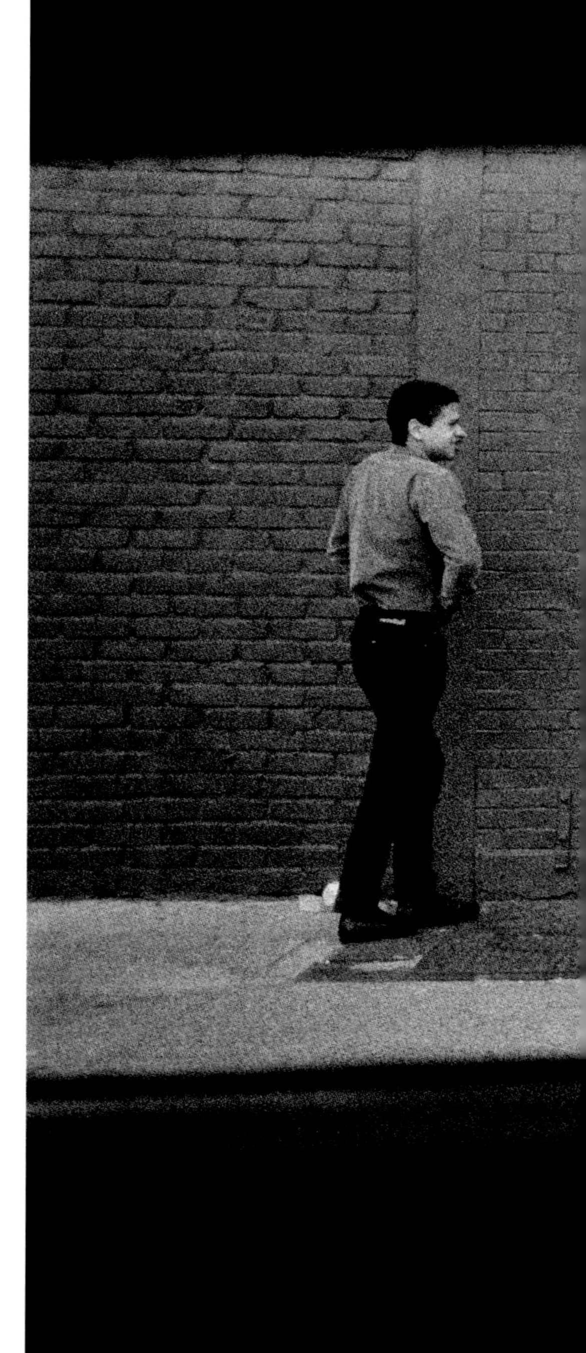

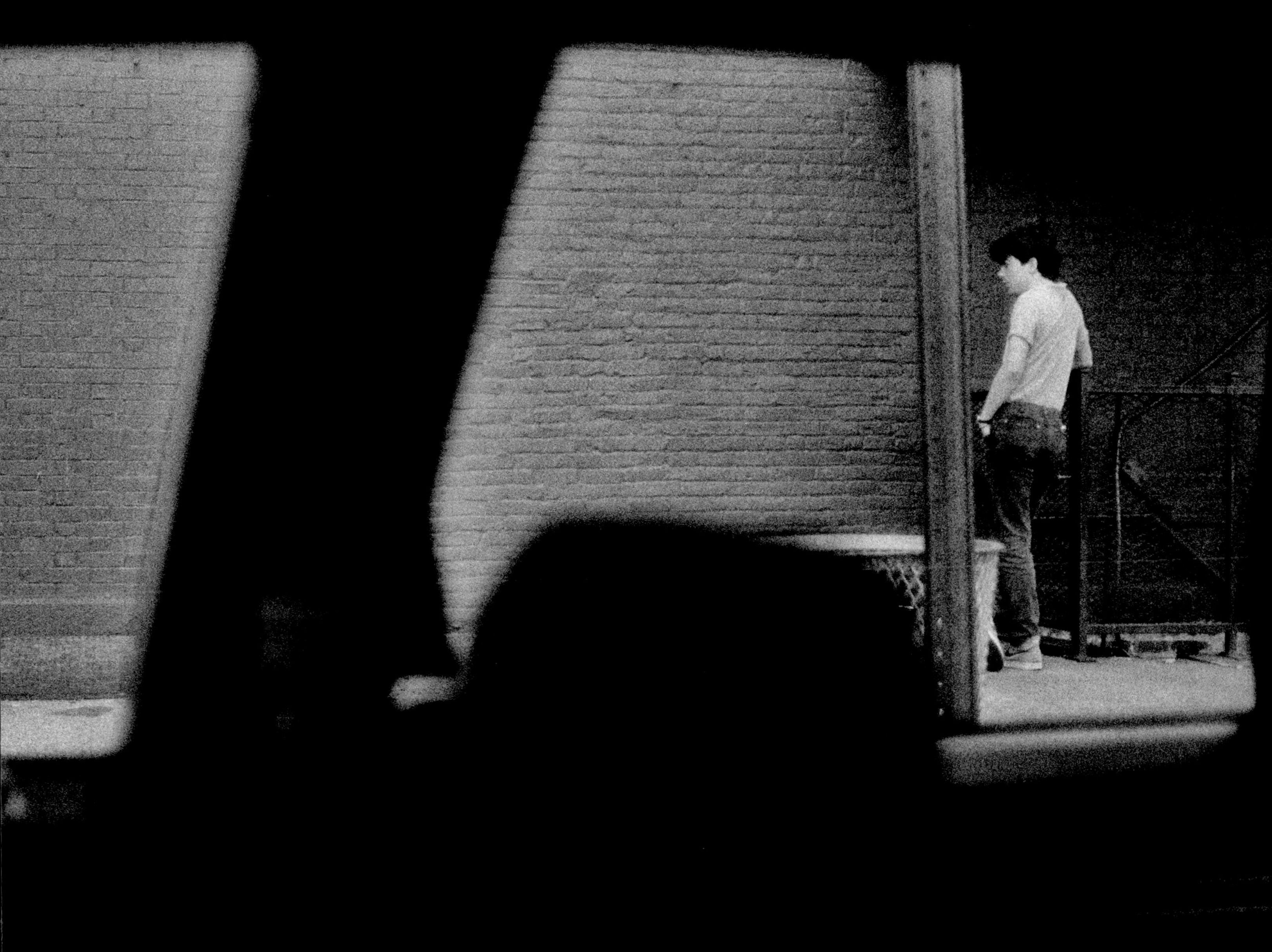

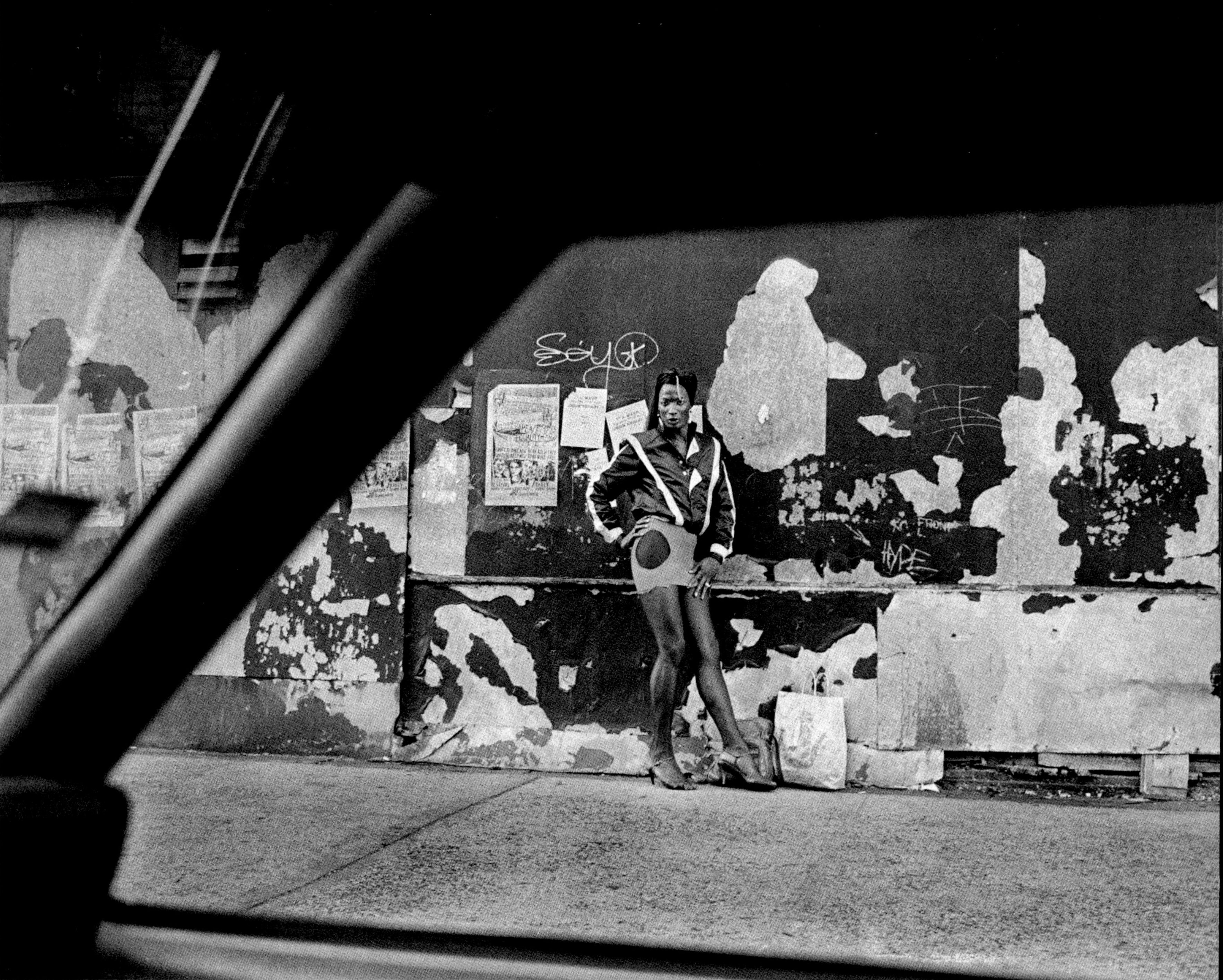
HYDE

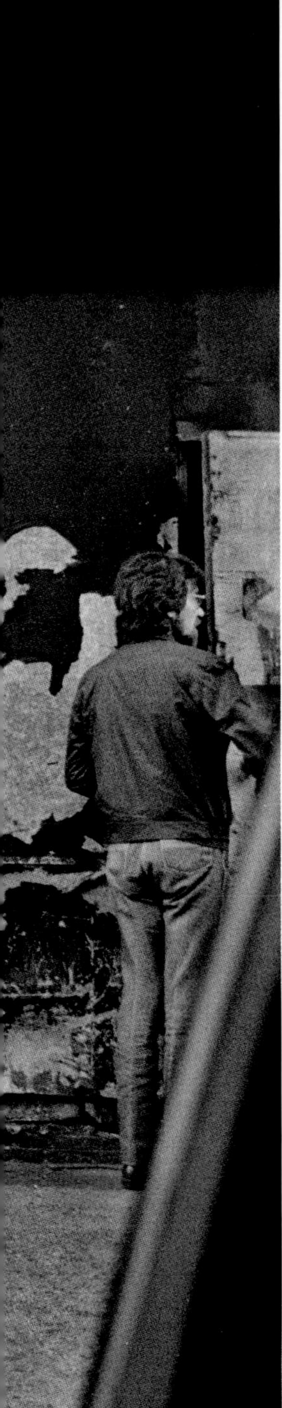

One morning, around 6:00 A.M., I was coming down Ninth Avenue near 46th Street, right by this bar where a lot of trans sex workers would hang out. I stopped at the light, and four six-foot-tall, size-12 high heel, smelling like macaroni egg salad, dirty, scuffed up knees, sex workers jump into my cab. Three in the back, one in the front. The one in the front slaps her hand down on my thigh, and says, “Oh, he’s cute,” while I’m trying to drive. Meanwhile, one of the three in the back starts screaming, “I was hustling that motherfucker, and you stole him!” at the one in the front, and sticks a knife through the window in the plastic shield, waving it all around. They’re screaming at each other, then suddenly it stops, and one of the others in the back says to me, “Hey, you know a good dope spot?”

I PULLED UP to this corner in the Meatpacking District, and I see a sex worker wearing a fur coat and heels. She walks over to the cab, opens her jacket, and is completely naked underneath.

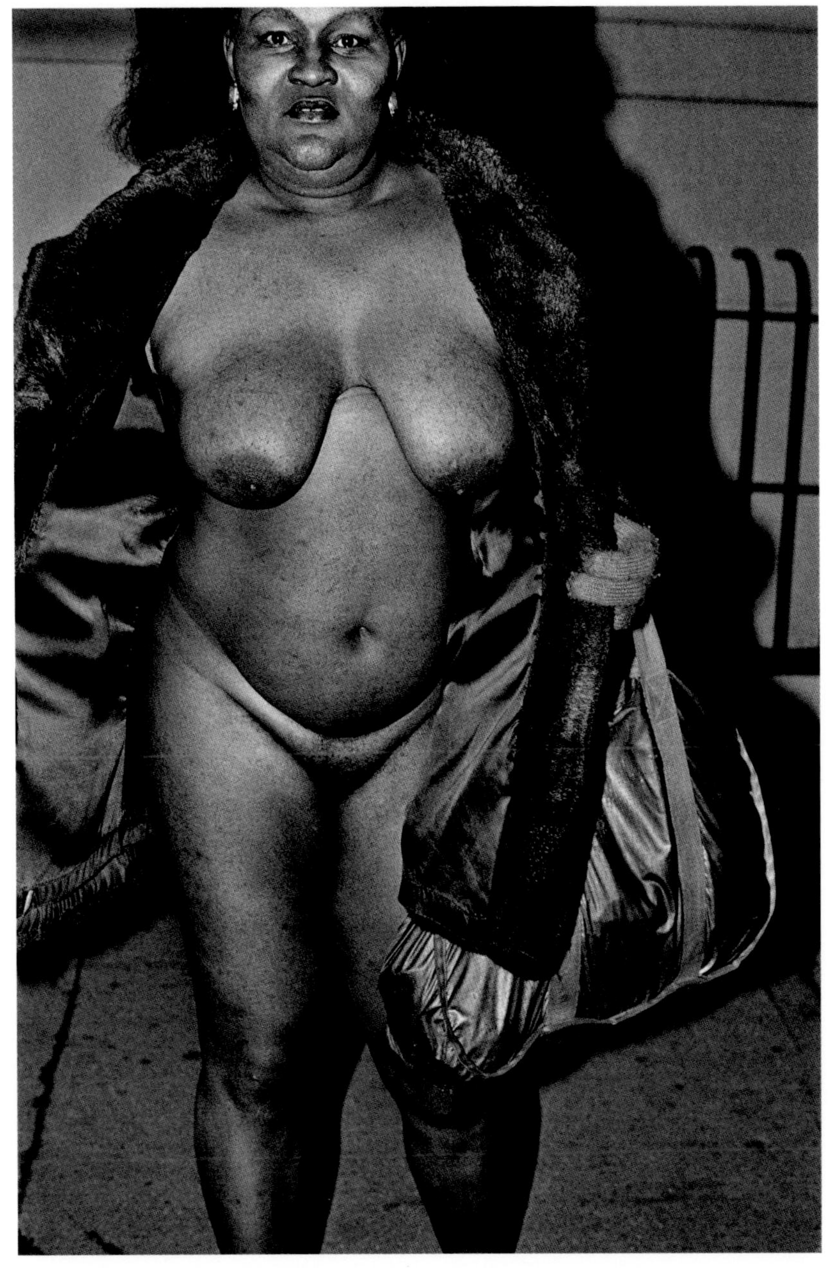

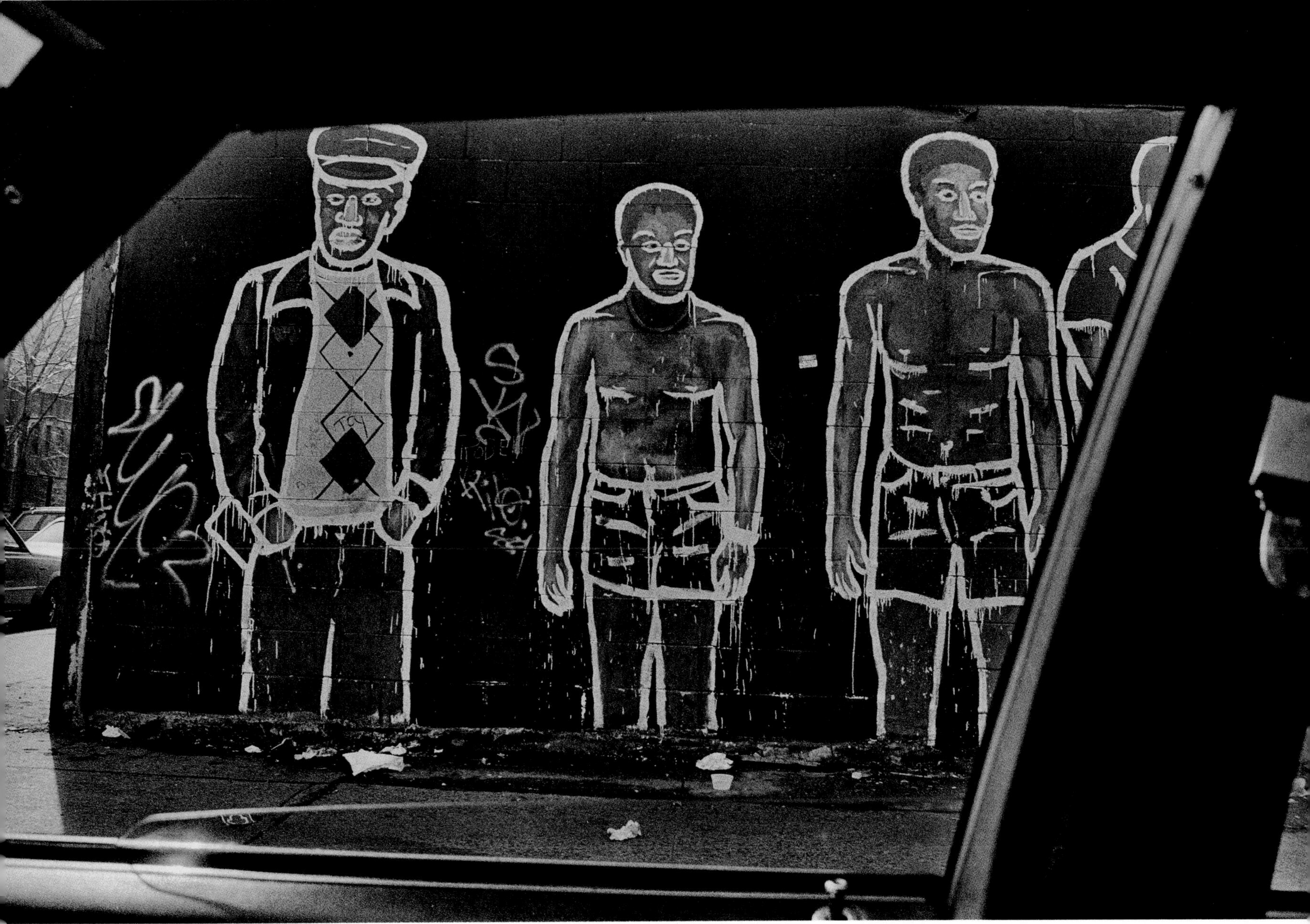

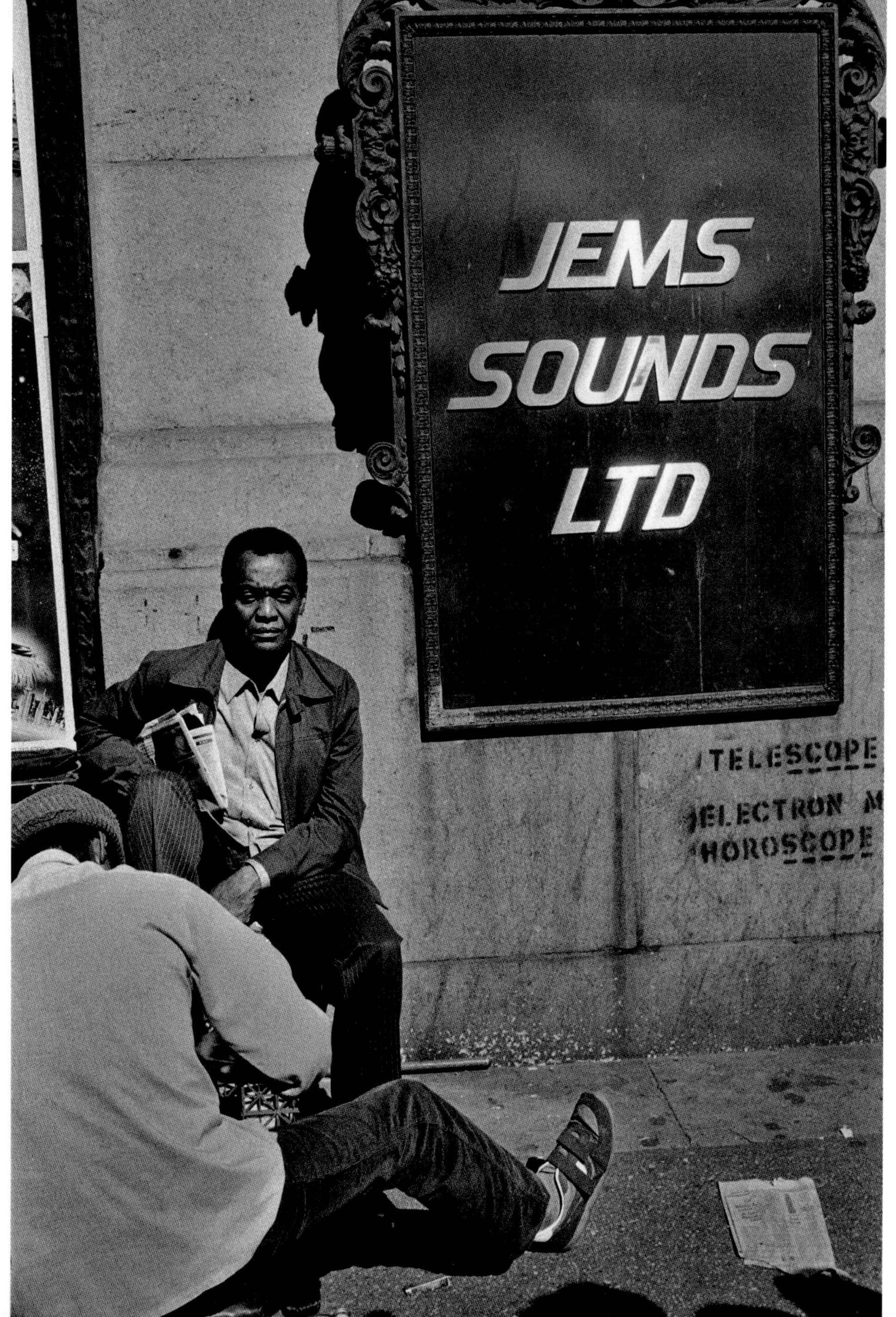
JEMS
SOUNDS
LTD
TELESCOPE
ELECTRON M
HOROSCOPE

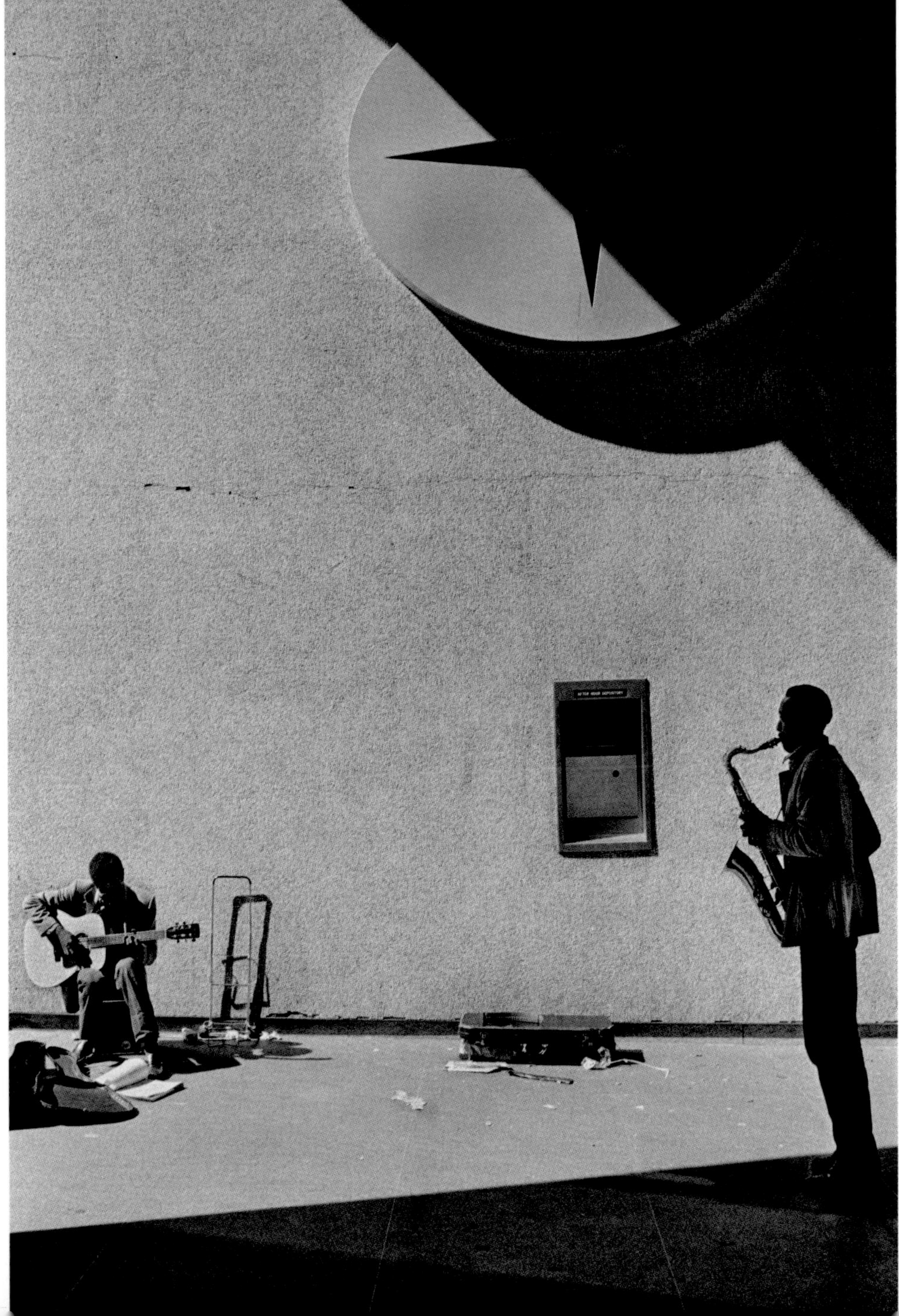

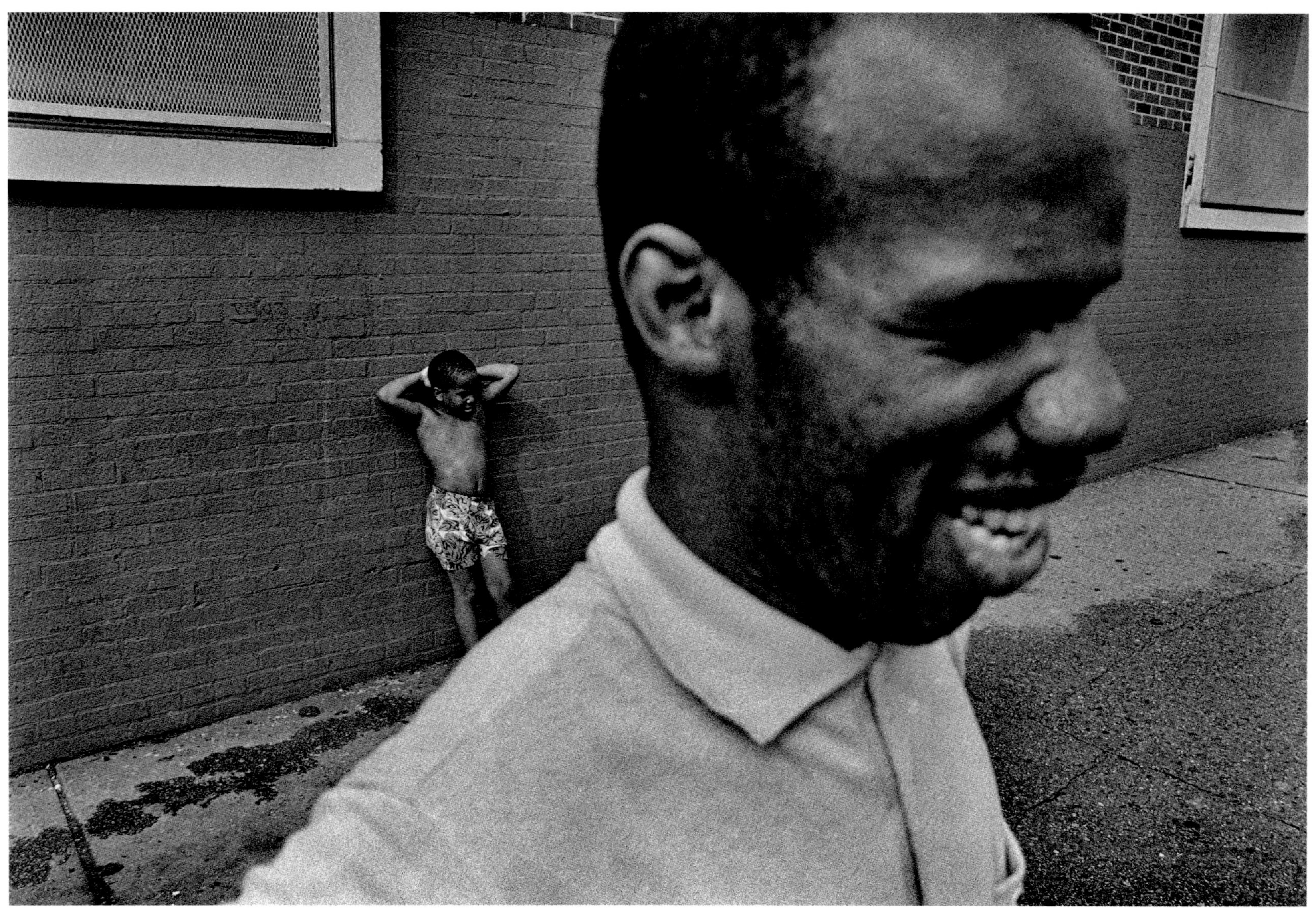

IN THE HEAT of the New York summer, driving a cab without air conditioning could be brutal. I was driving down Second Avenue, and saw these kids keeping cool with an open fire hydrant. I pulled over and cooled down with them.

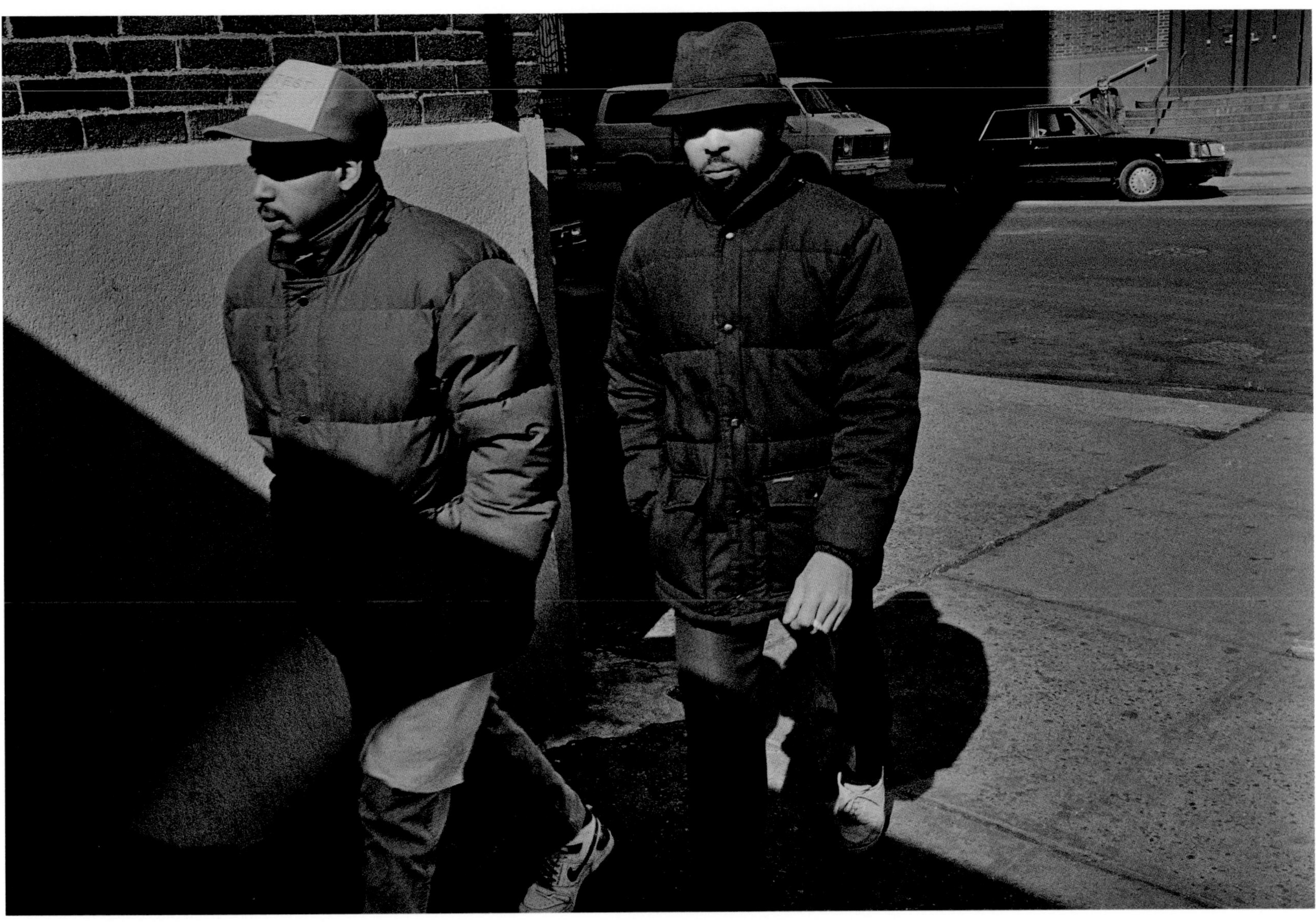

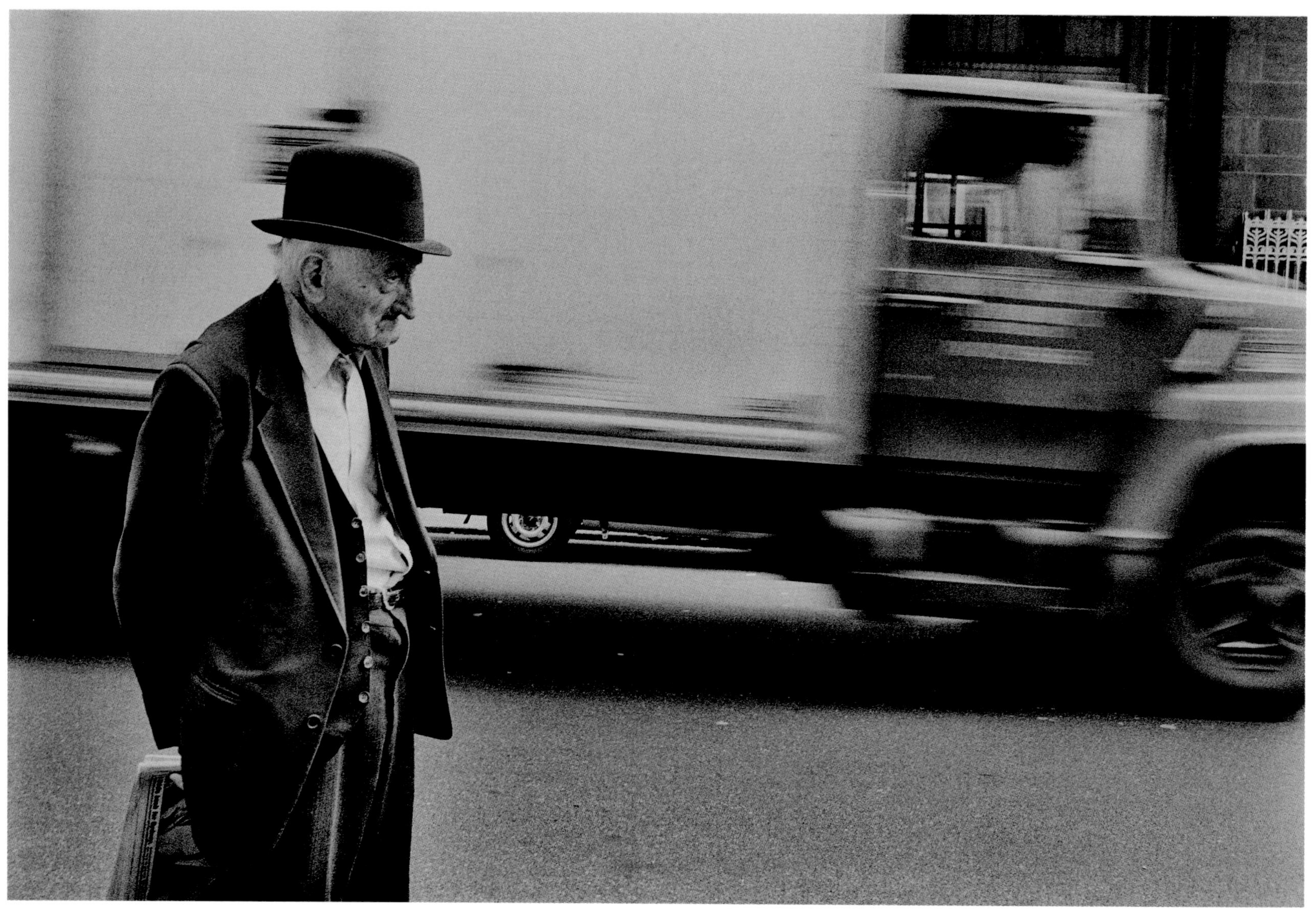

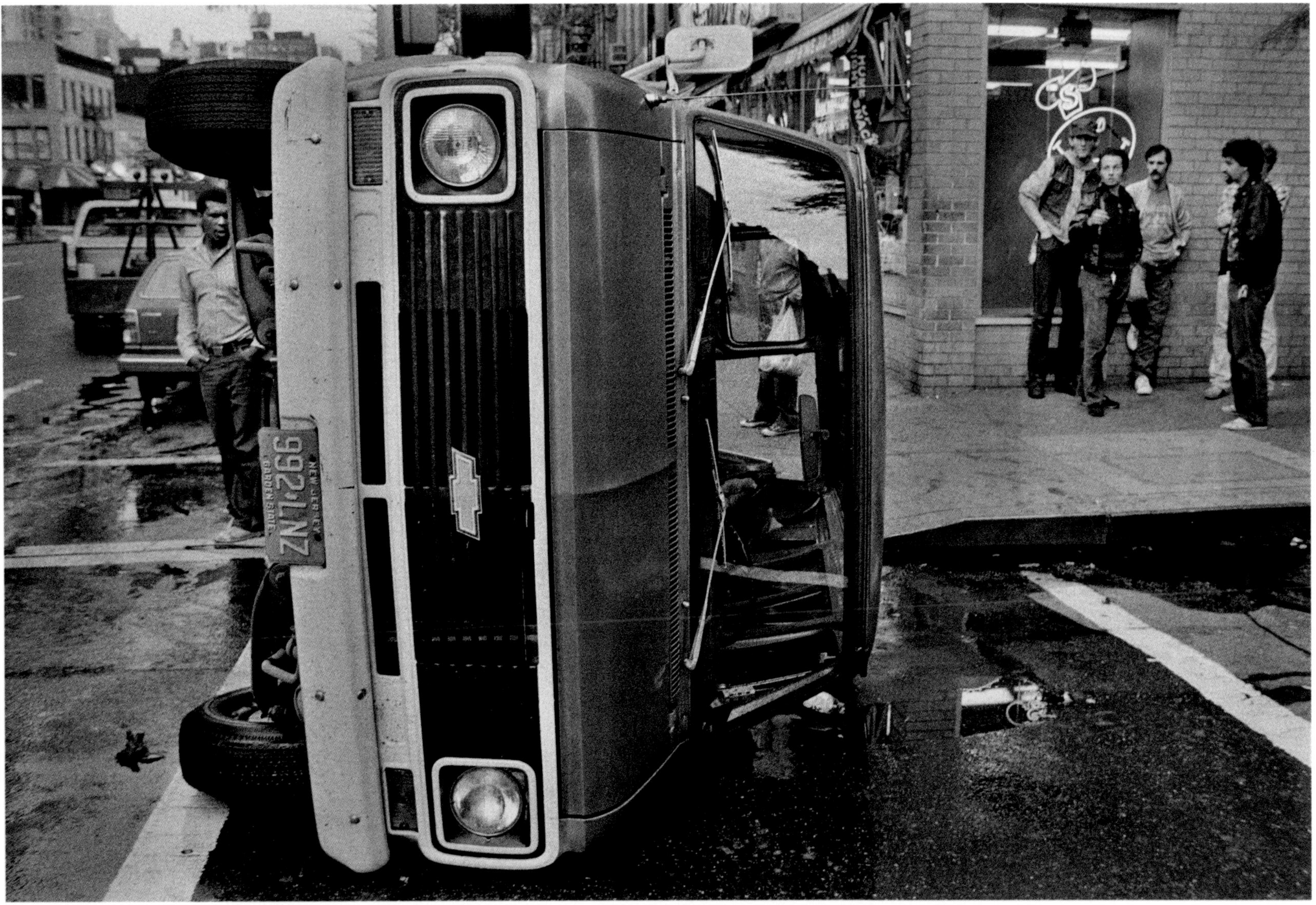
NEW JERSEY
992·LNZ
GARDEN STATE

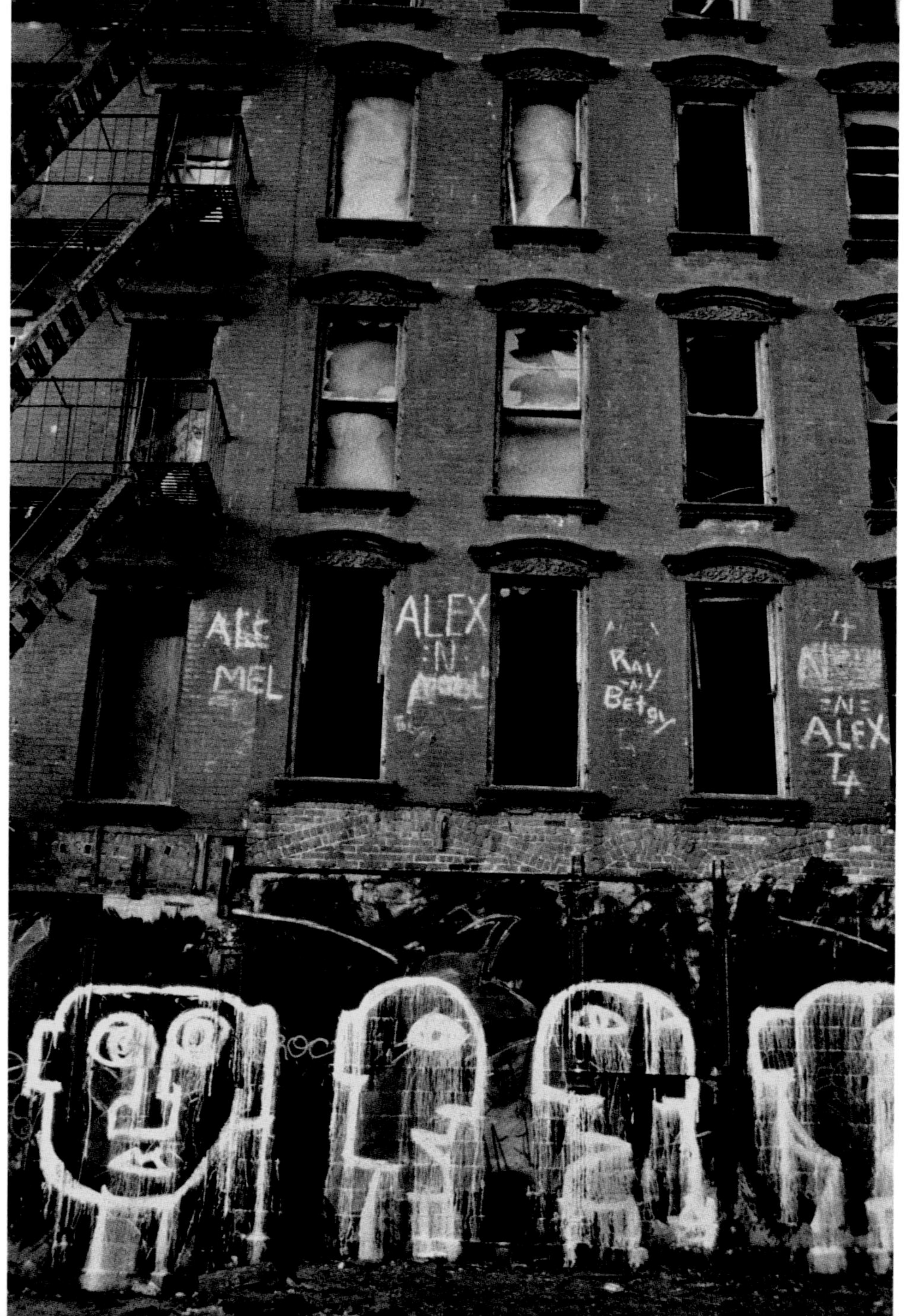
MEL
ALEX
N
Ray
N
Betsy
N
ALEX

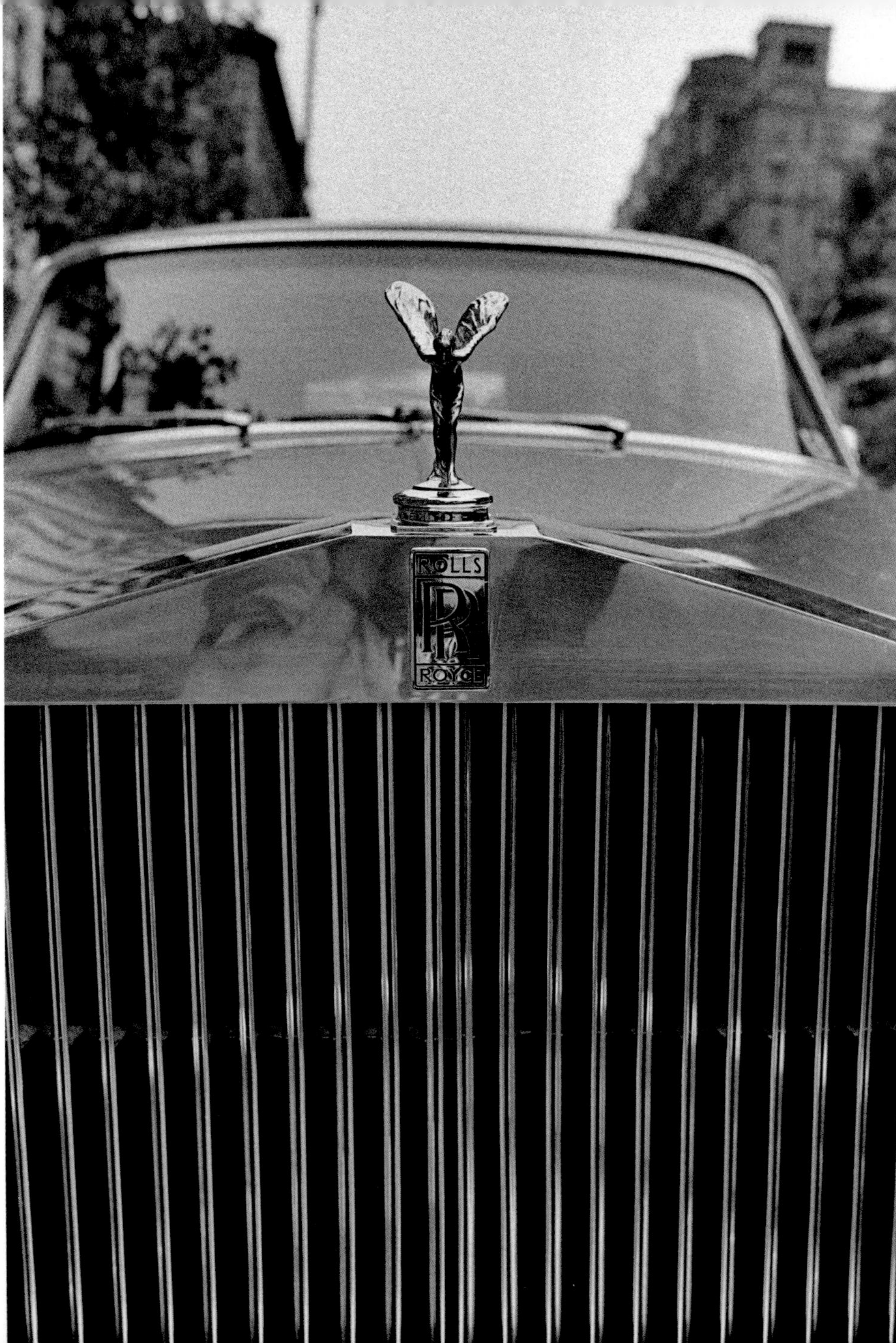
ROLLS
RR
ROYCE

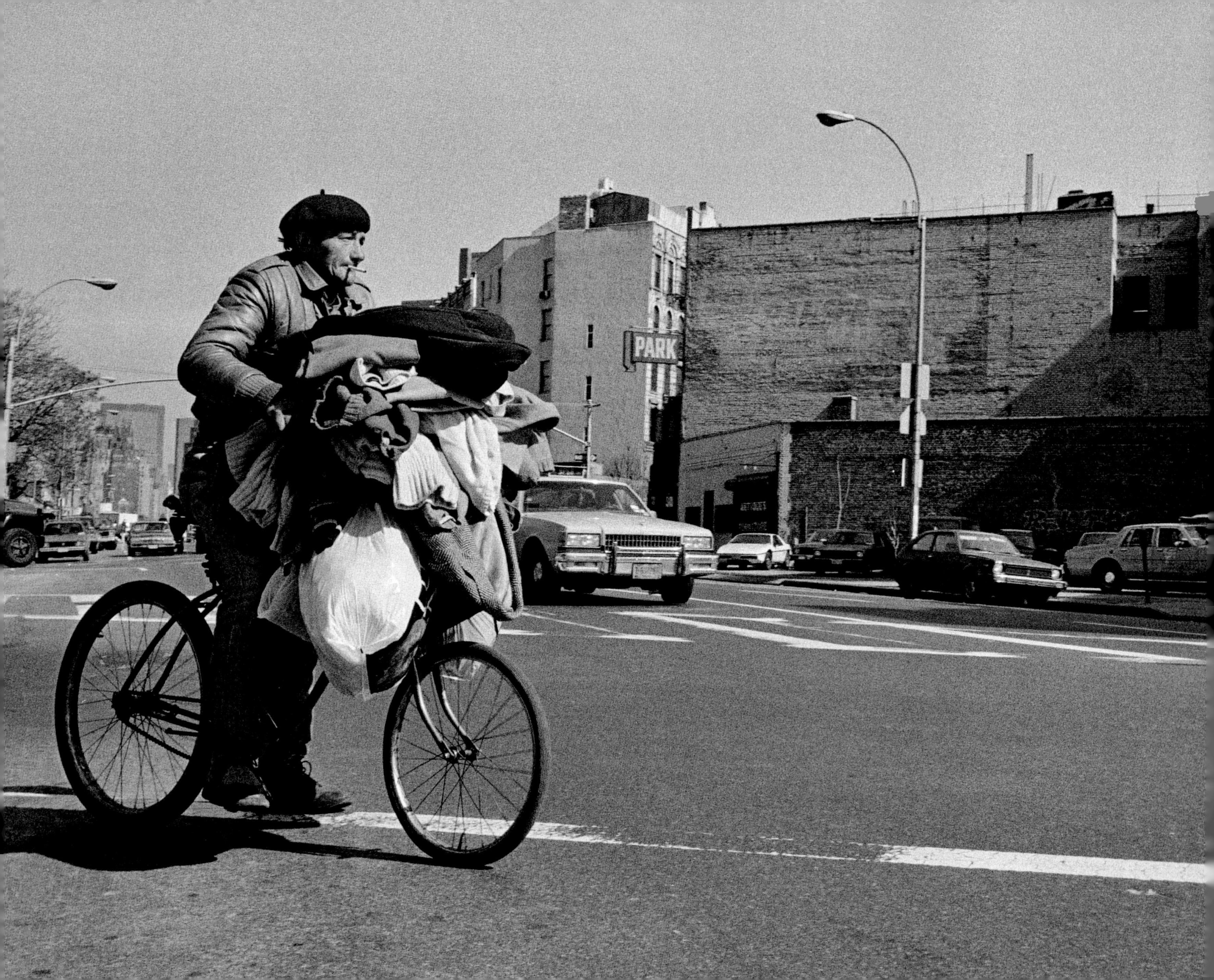
PARK

THIS WAS THE END of the SRO (single room occupancy) hotels. A lot of people on the edge would live in SROs. All the way uptown, and all the way downtown. Then they started warehousing the properties to make them all upscale like you have today. The SROs were a huge safety net for people at the bottom. Once they were taken away, a lot of people ended up on the street.

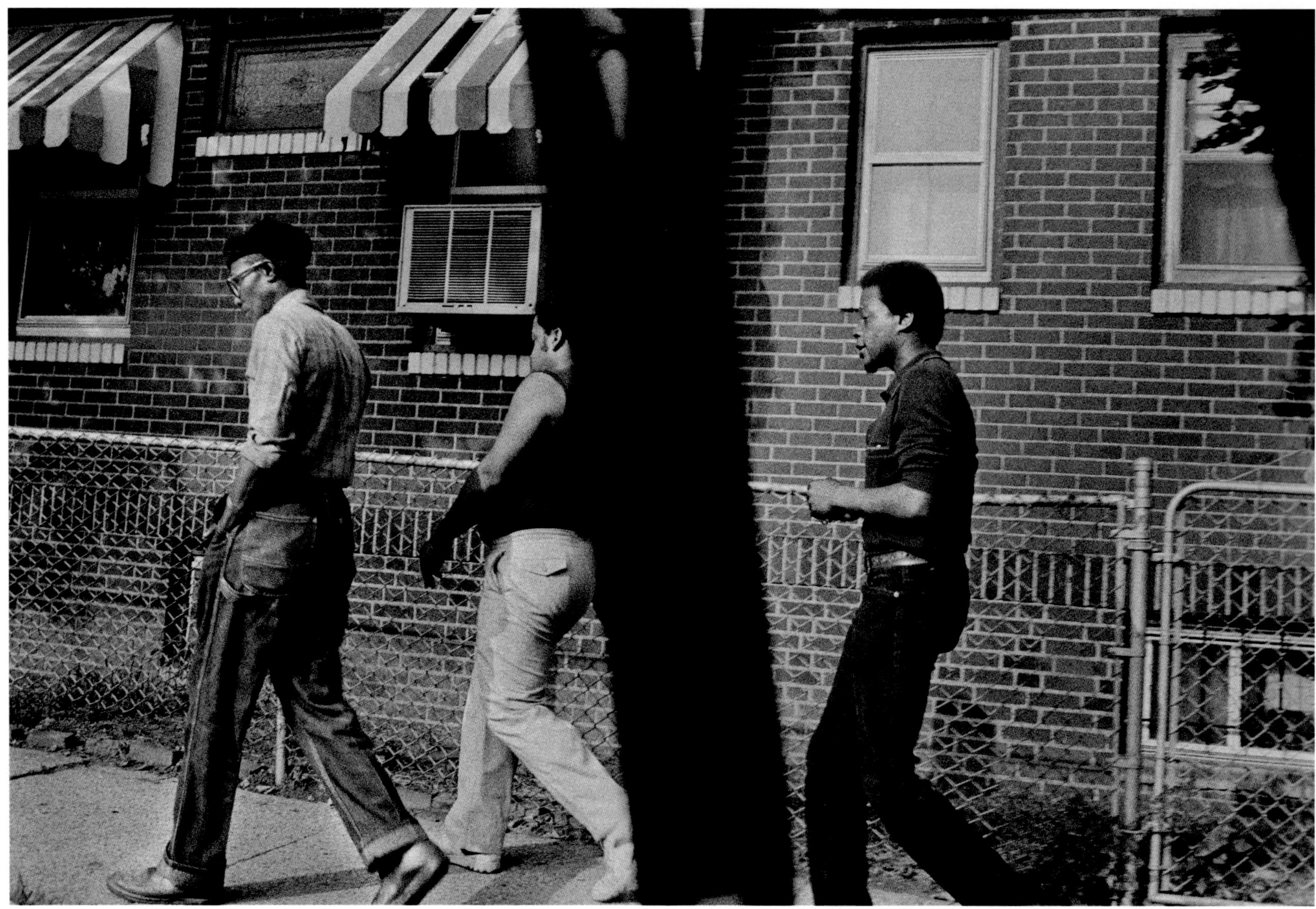

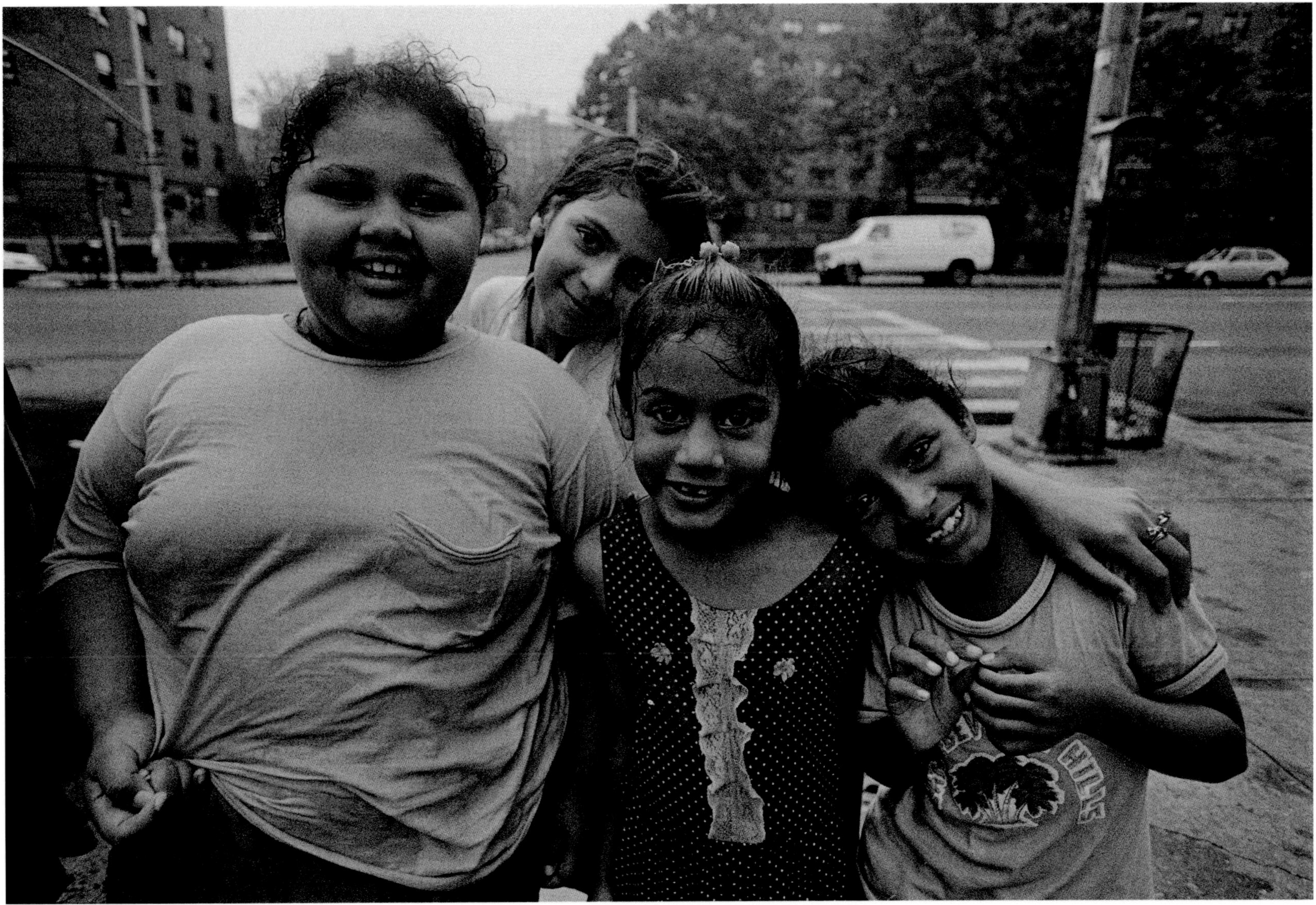

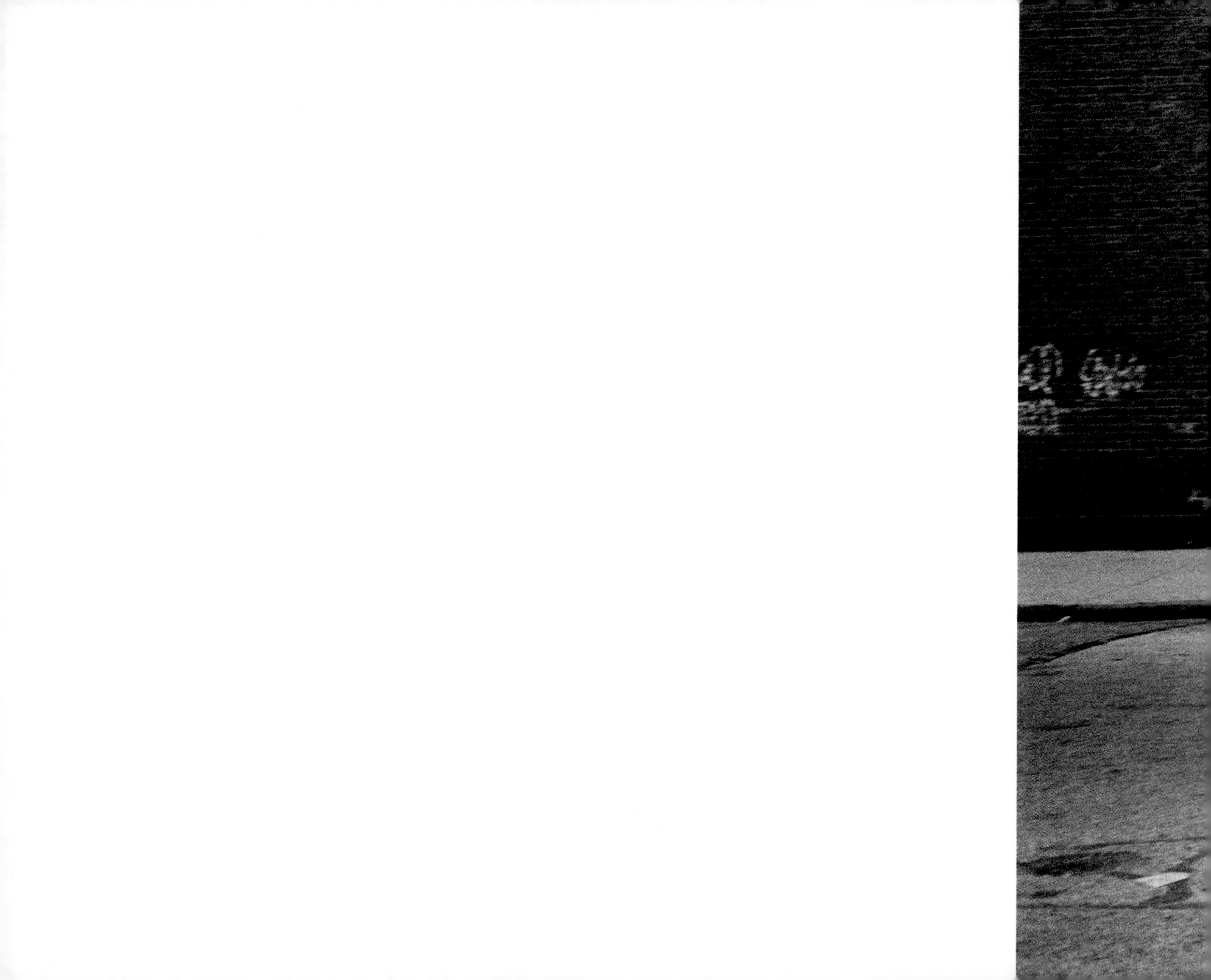

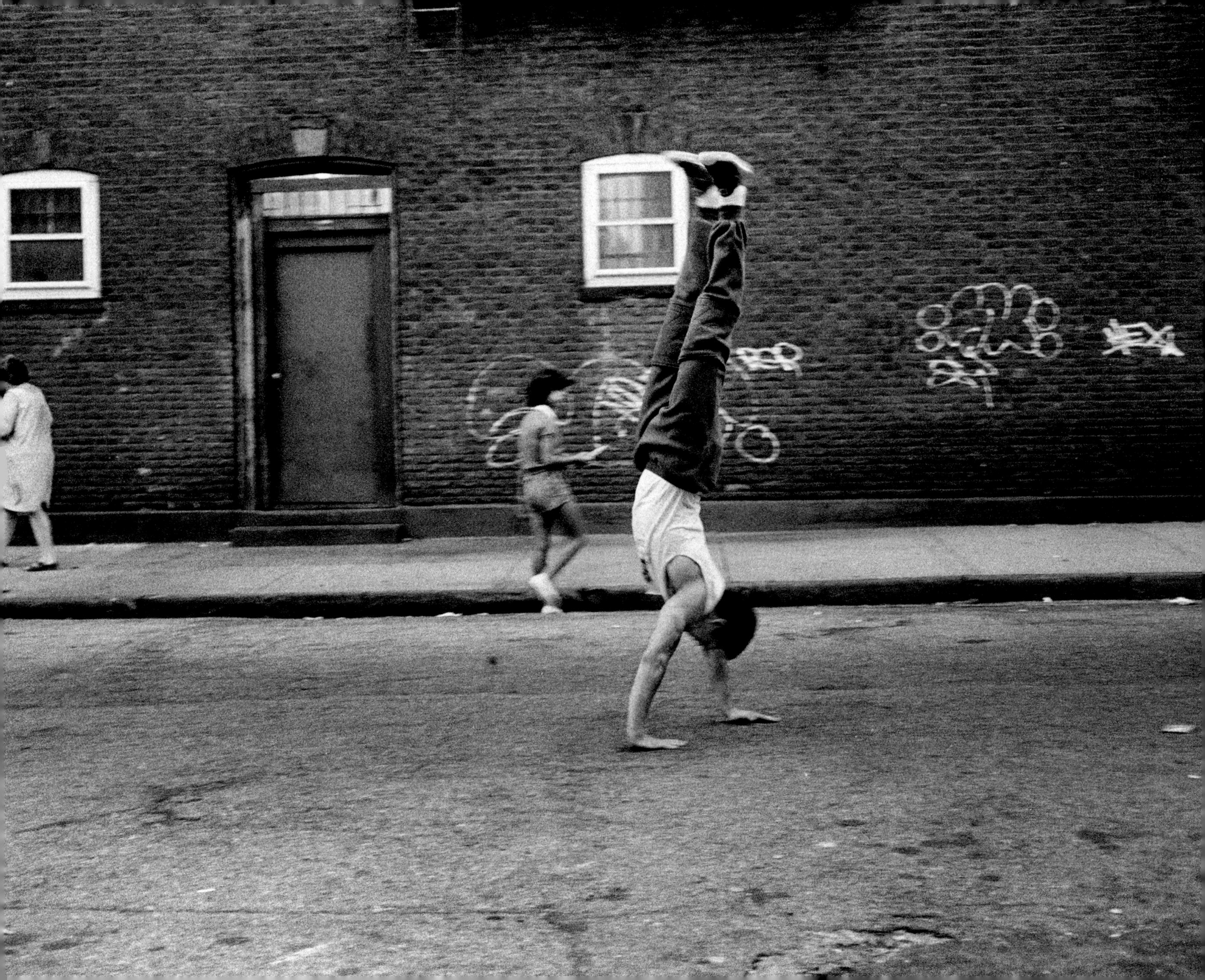

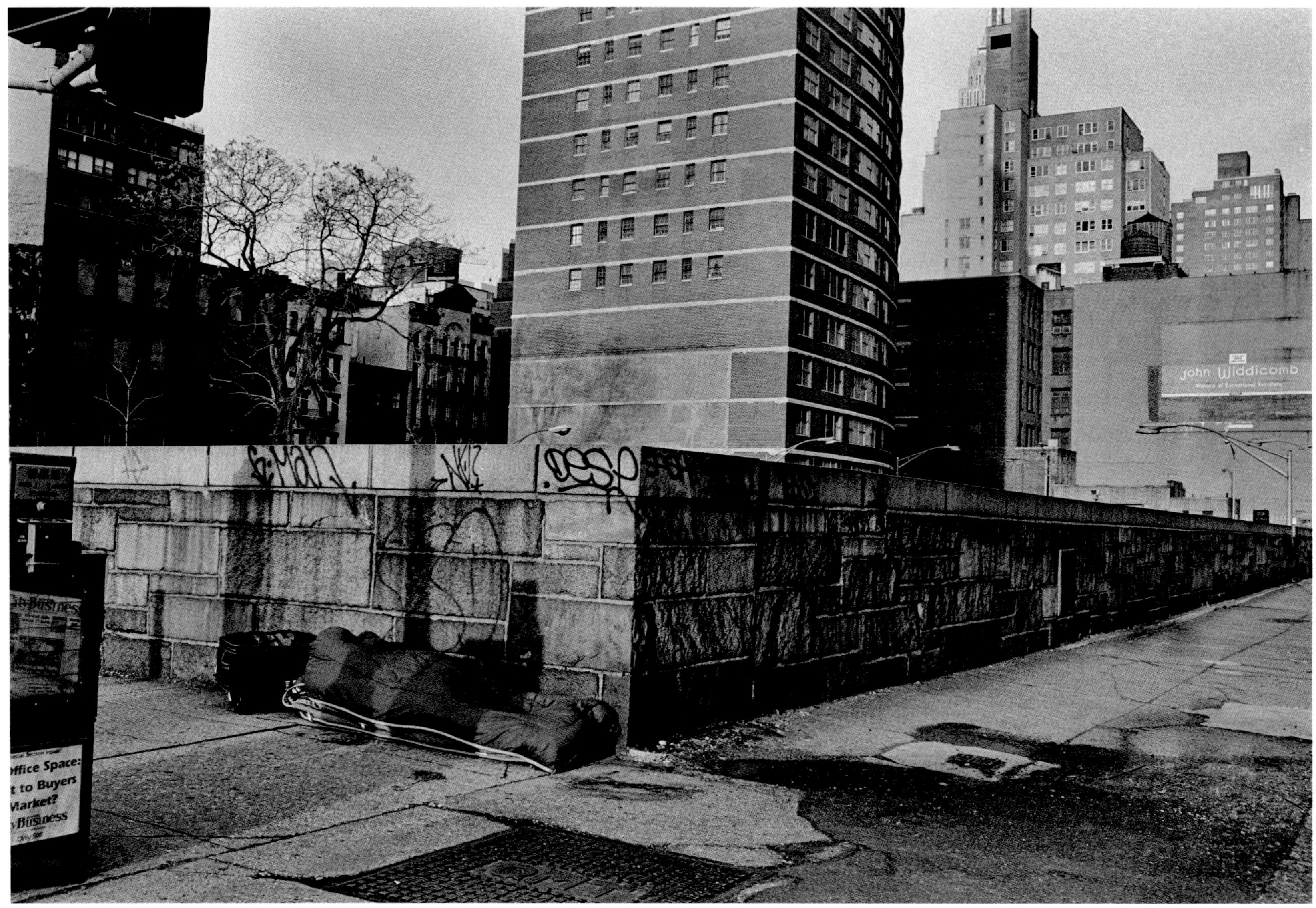
john Widdicomb
Office Space:
t to Buyers
Market?

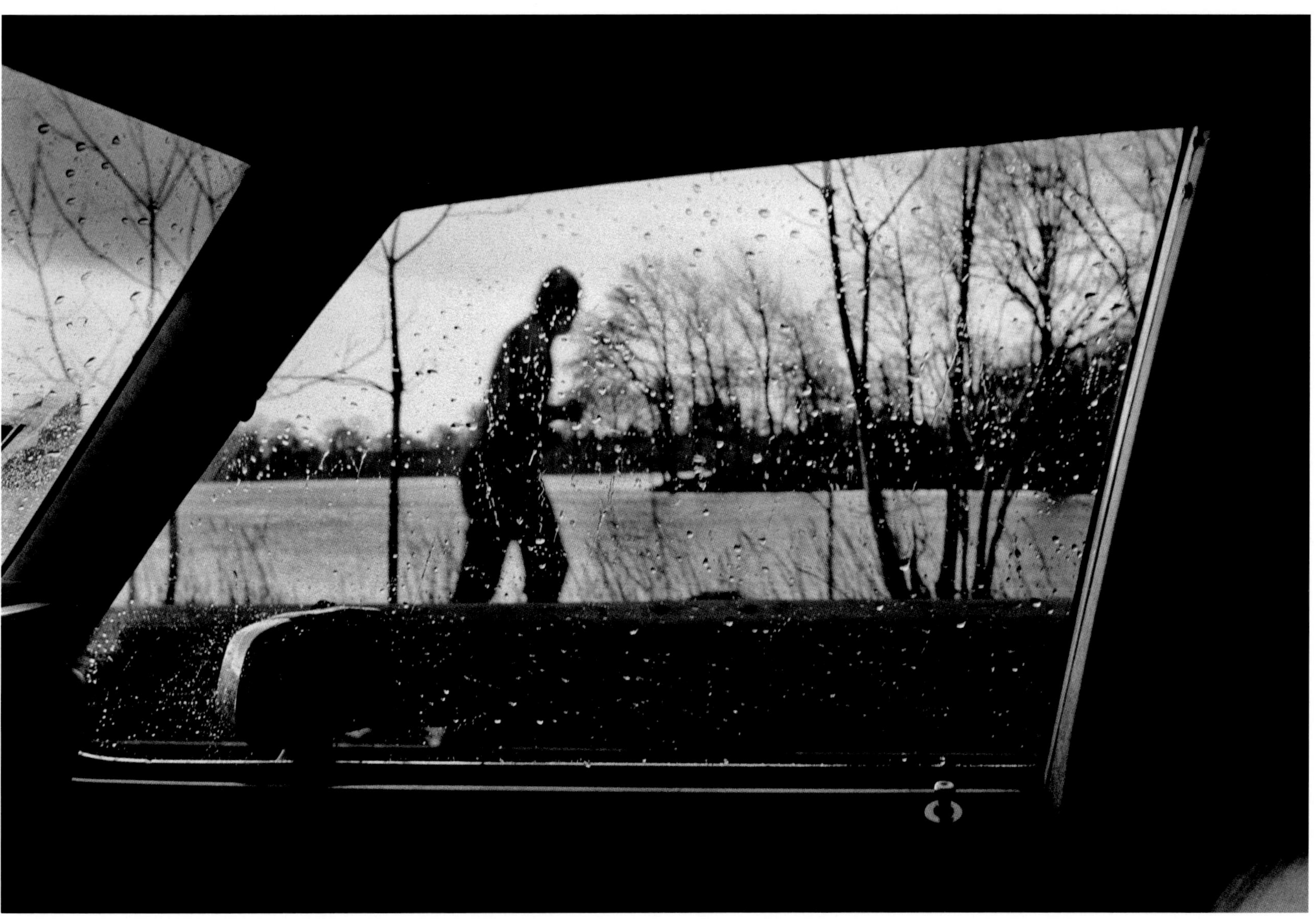

YOU NEVER KNEW who your next fare would be.

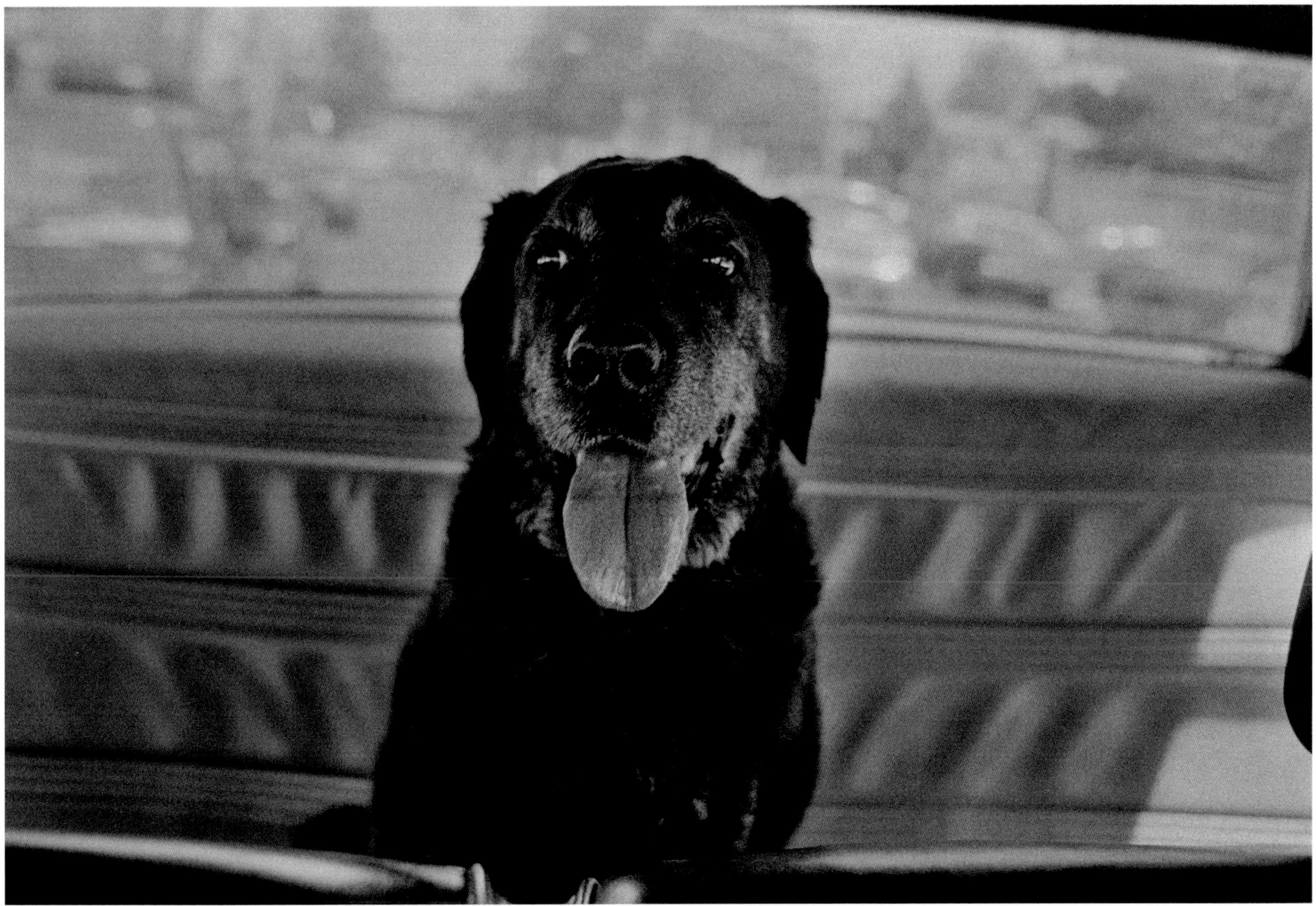

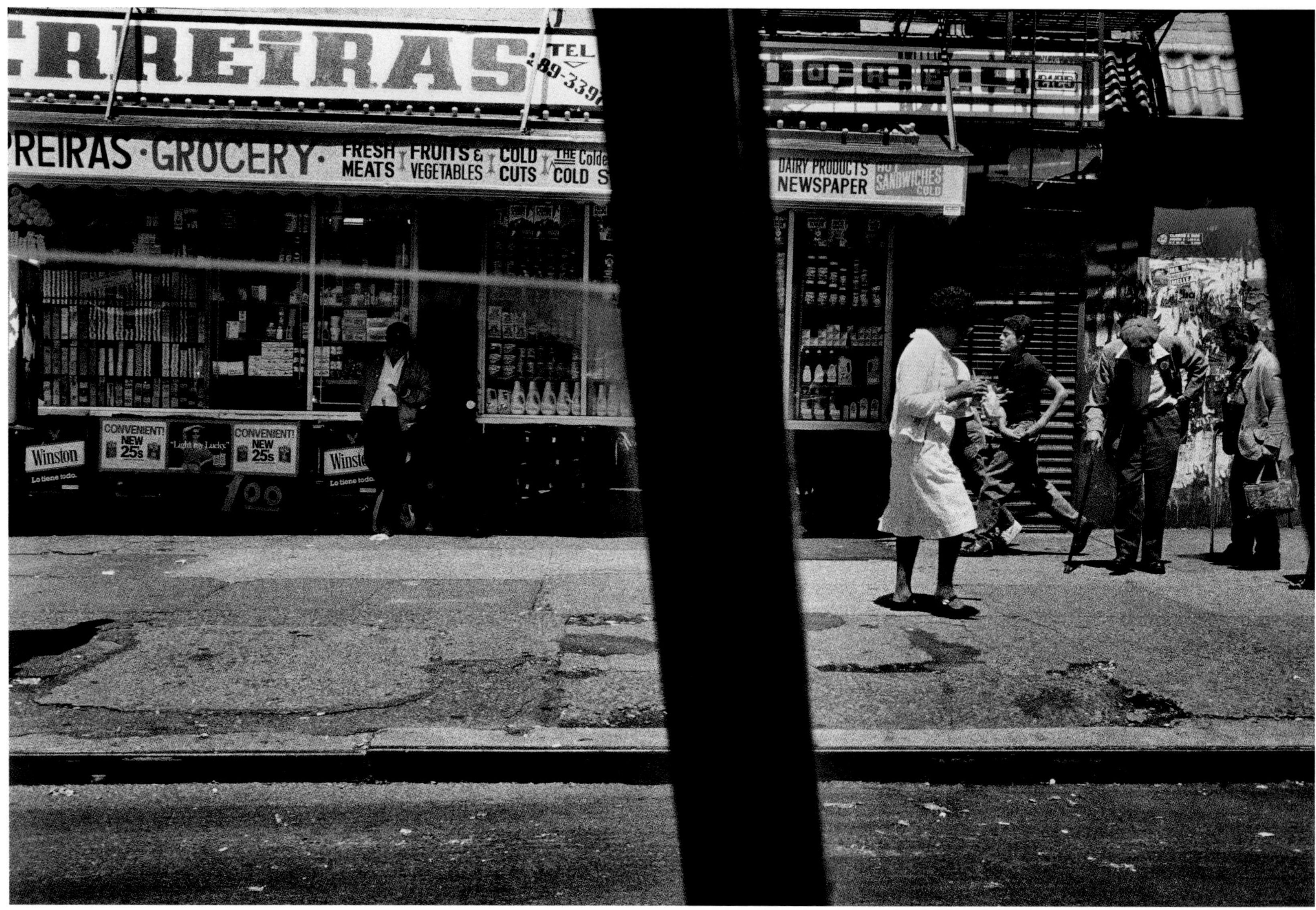
RREIRAS
TEL
PREIRAS · GROCERY ·
FRESH MEATS
FRUITS & VEGETABLES
COLD CUTS
DAIRY PRODUCTS
NEWSPAPER
HOT SANDWICHES COLD
CONVENIENT! NEW 25's
CONVENIENT! NEW 25's
Winston
Lo tiene todo.

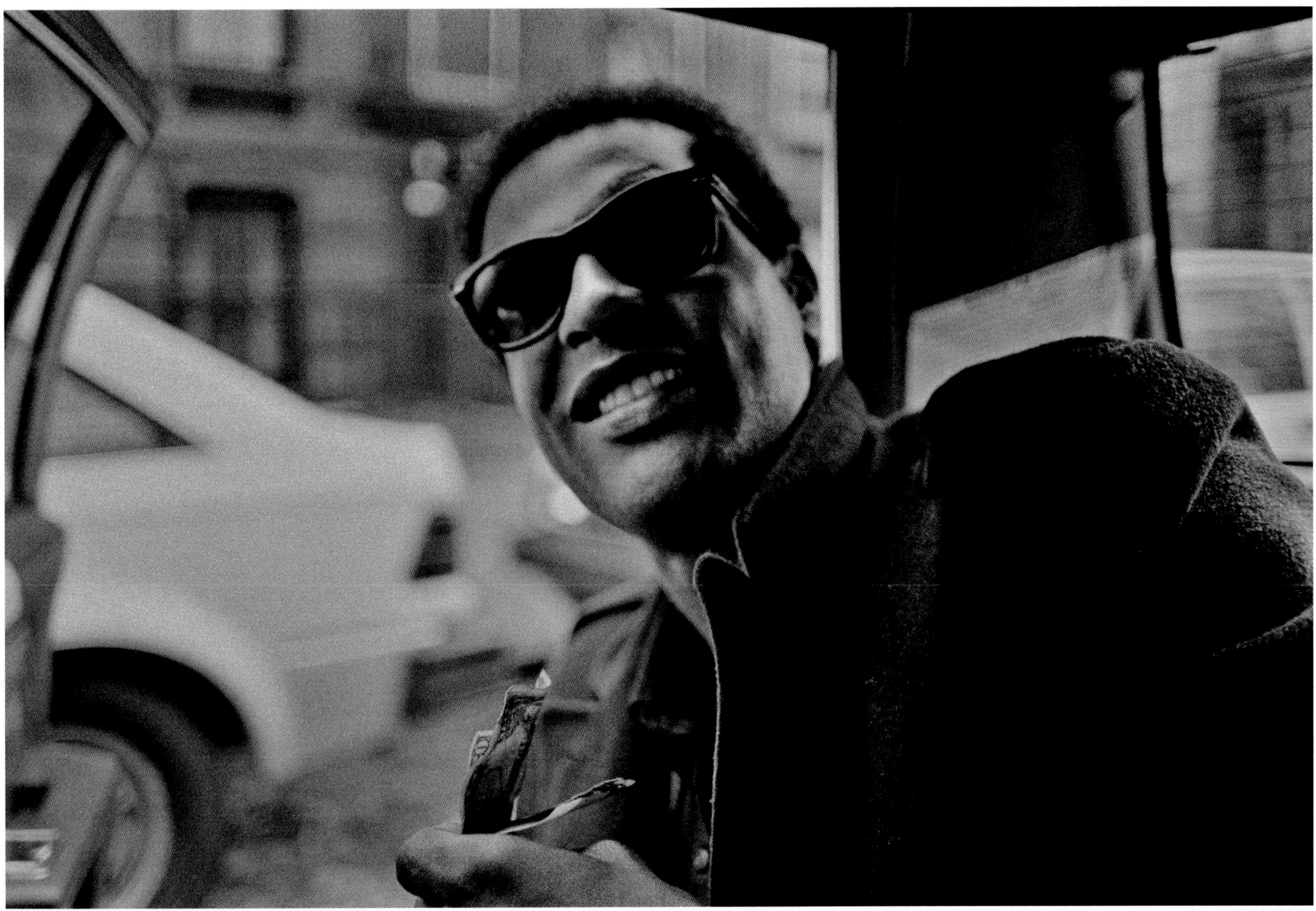

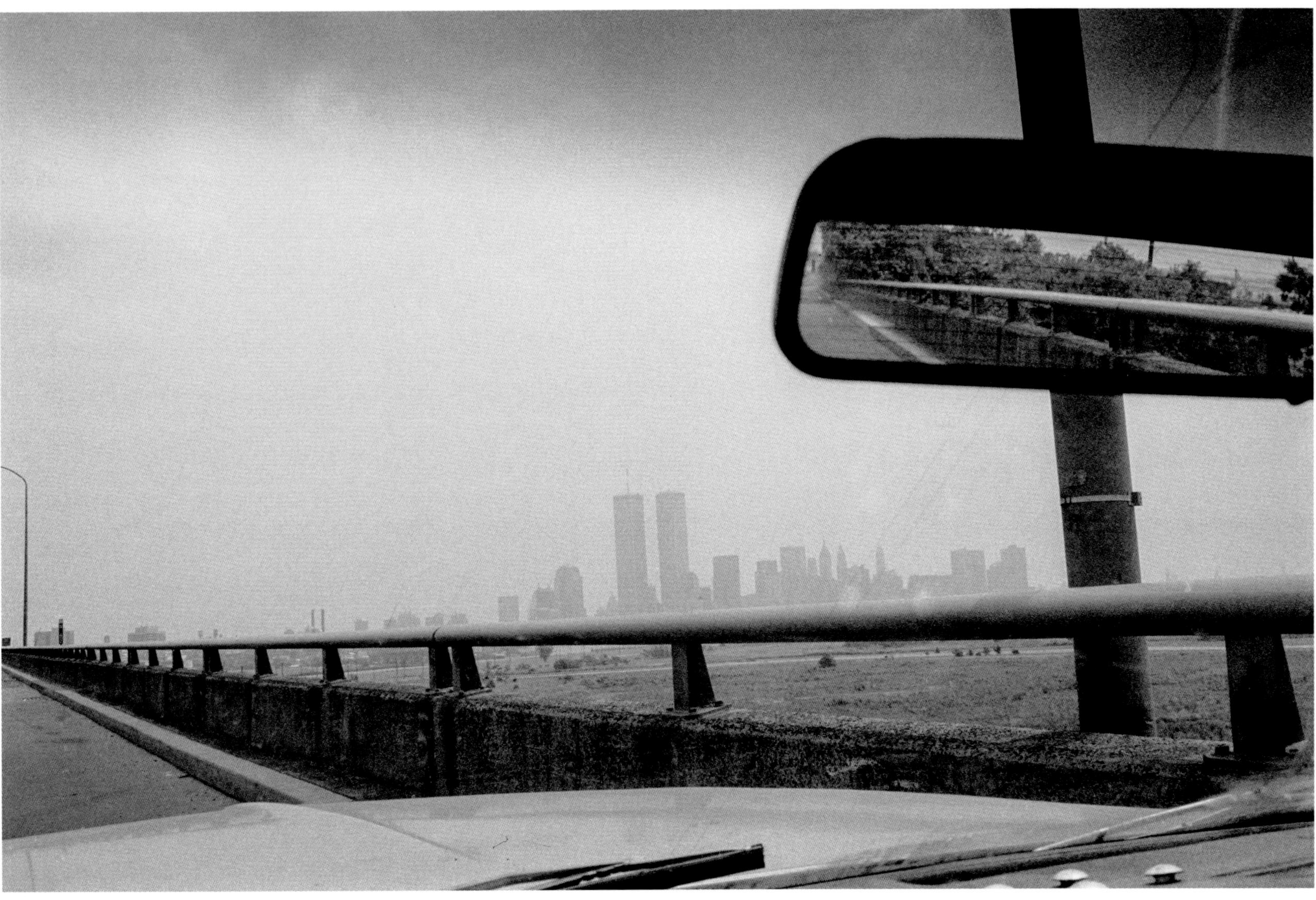

Aknowledgements:

I would like to thank my mother Carmen who worked so hard to raise me right and taught me the importance of listening and looking.

My deepest gratitude to Richard Price for his soulful essay.

A special thank you to Greg Alders for his post production.

I am very thankful to Andy Outis for his time, expertise and design with this book.

Bene Taschen and his gallery for supporting and representing my work.

To Blur, a student publication of the International Center of Photography Education Department.

A special thank you to Daniel Power and the powerHouse team for publishing this work.

Finally, I would like to sincerely thank my city and its people of New York which have given so much to me as a photographer.

CAPTIONS

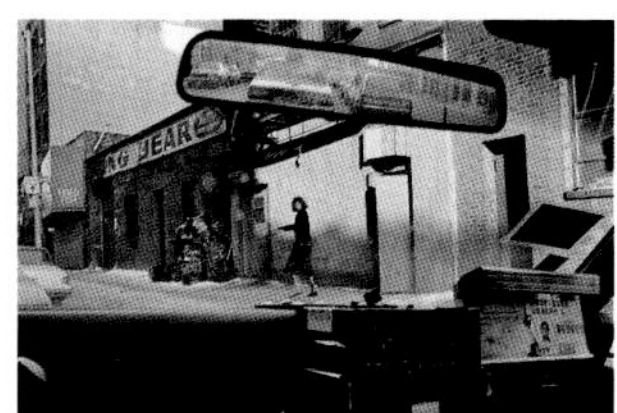

220 West Houston Street

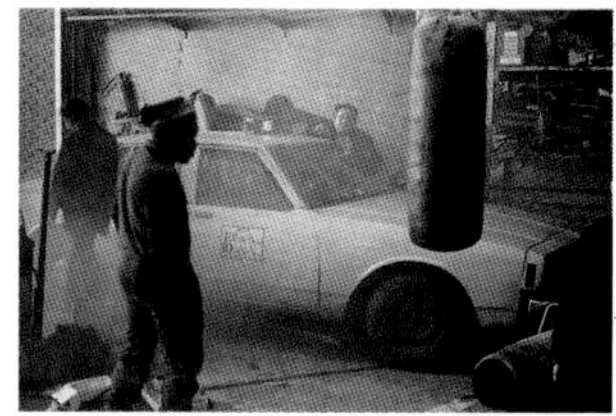

At the garage, my cab broke down

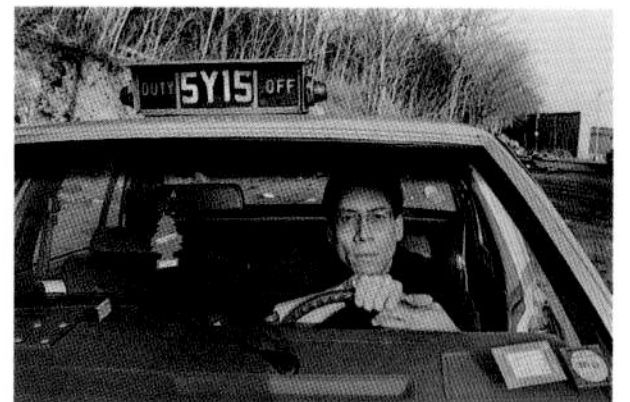

Self portrait

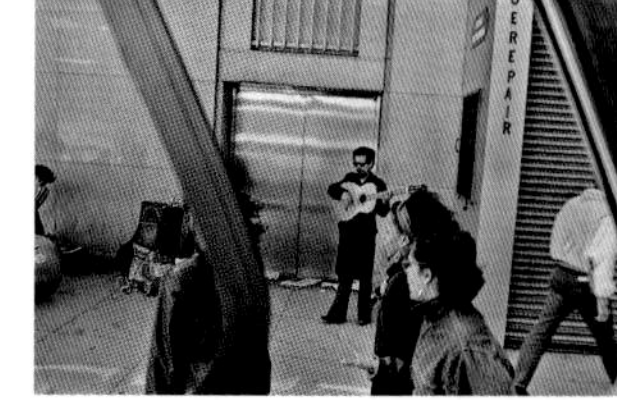

Times Square

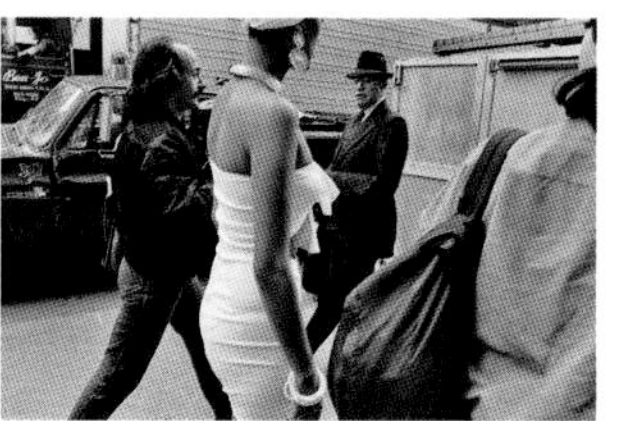

Midtown

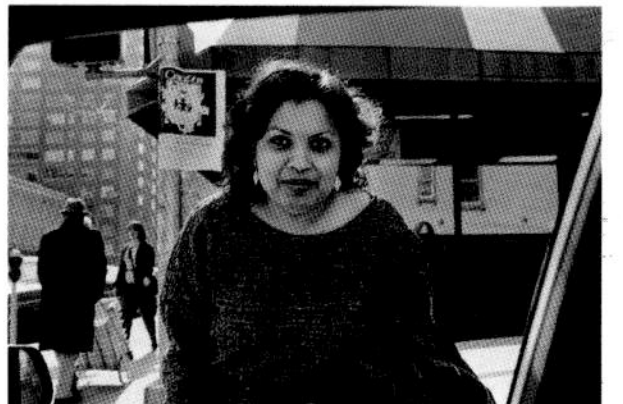

Untitled

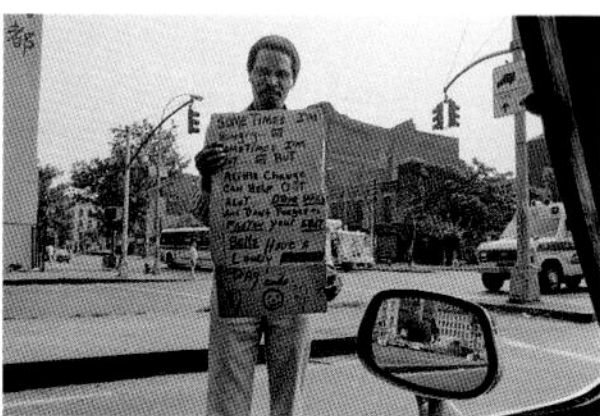

A panhandler at Bowery & Houston, East Village

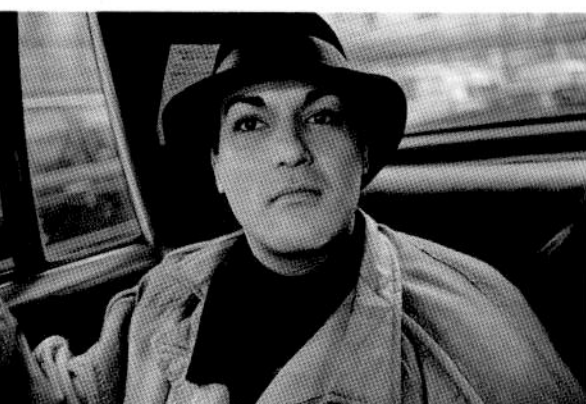

Meat Packing District, I picked him up from one of the clubs. He was a drag performer, and I was taking him home to Brooklyn.

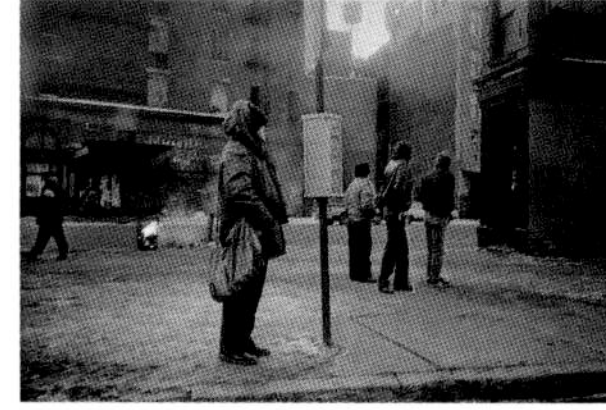

Greenwich Village

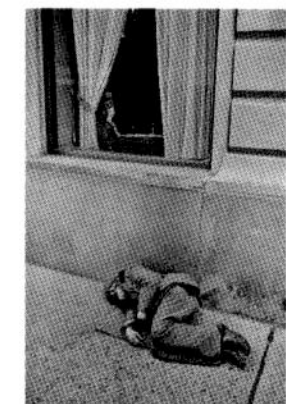

Park Avenue, Kips Bay

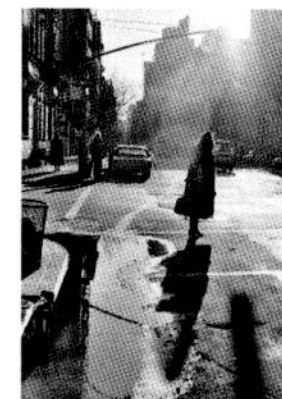

Waiting for a cab

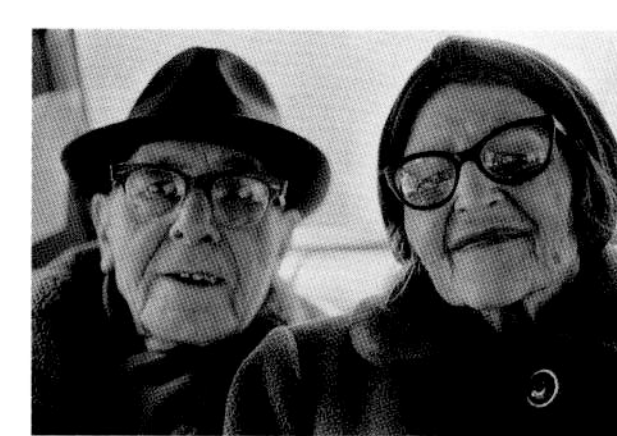

Manhattan

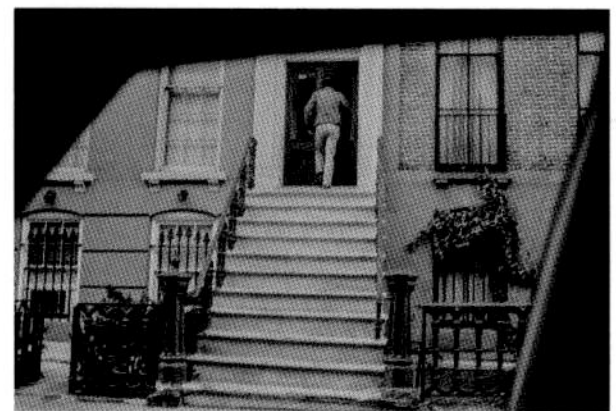

Untitled

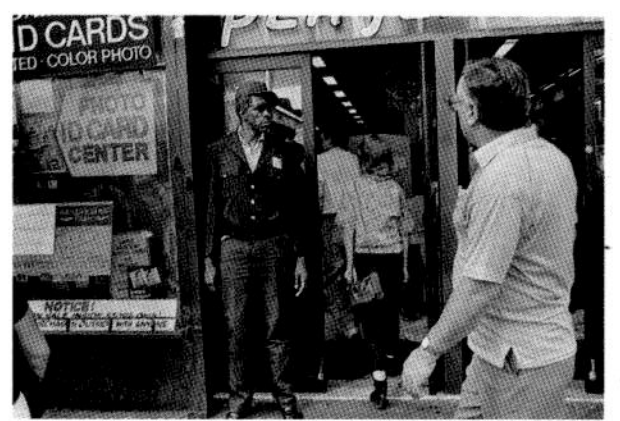

Times Square

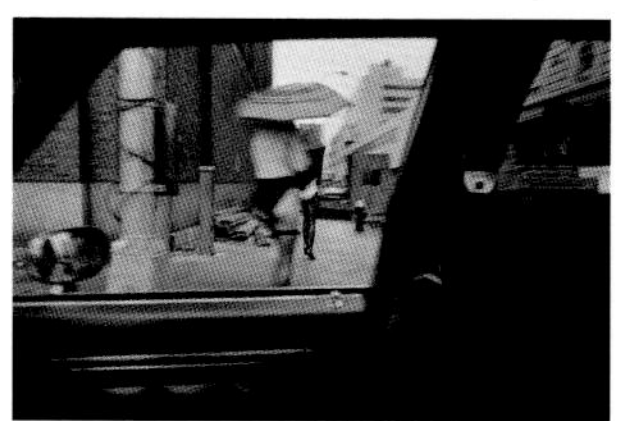

Hell's Kitchen

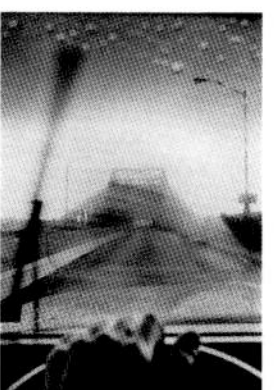

Pulaski Skyway, New Jersey

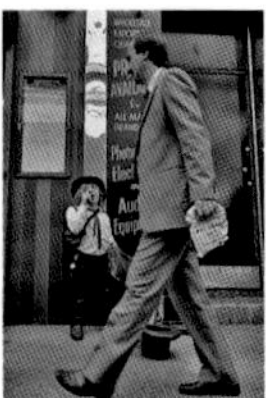
14th Street

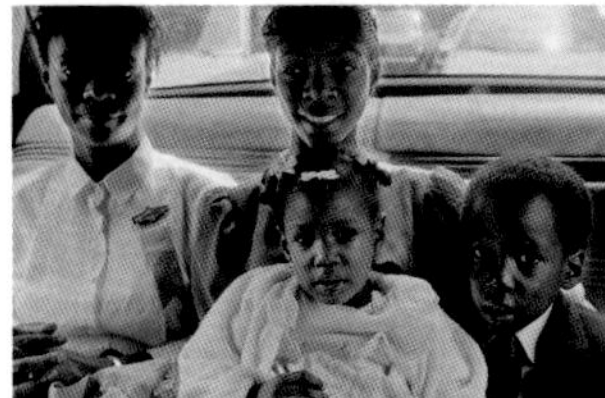
Family going to church on a Sunday morning

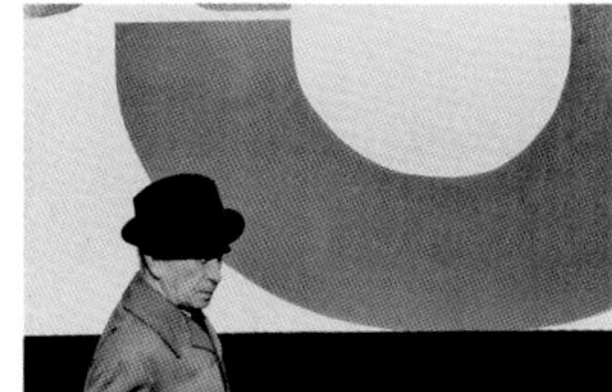
Midtown

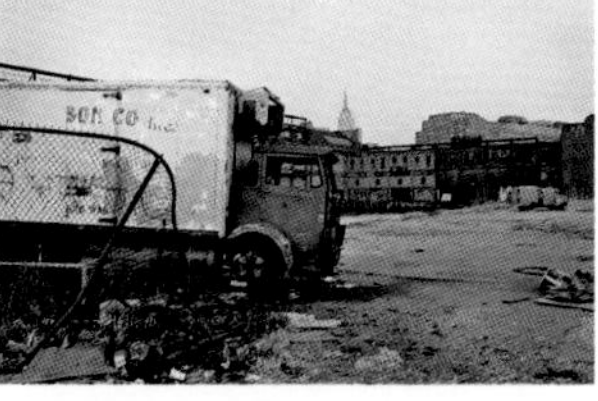
Greenwich Village, West Side Highway, around 10th Street. It was just empty lots. Trucks from all over the city would park there. And that's where a lot of gay men would cruise.

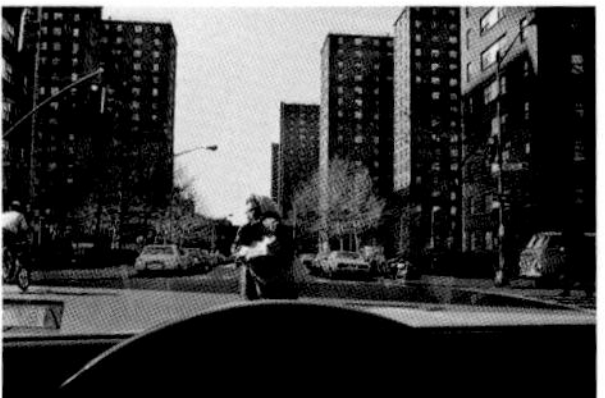
East Harlem

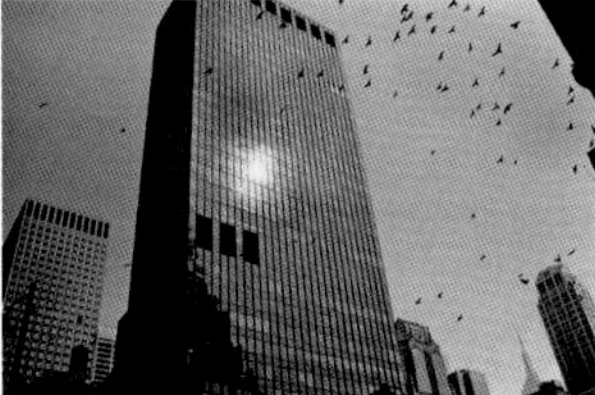
Birds over Midtown

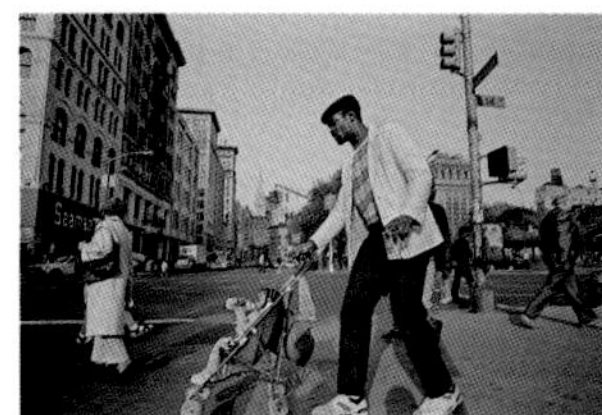
Union Square

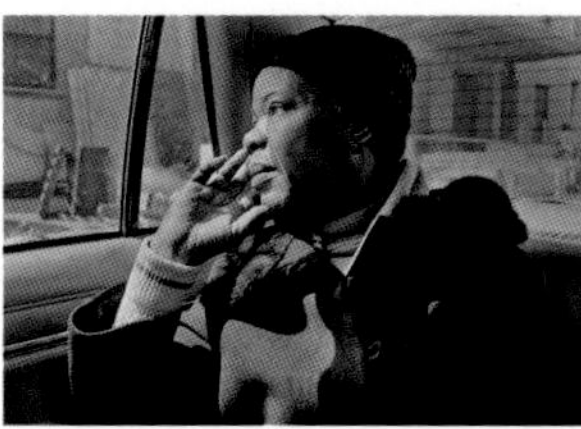
This woman was talking to me about her neighborhood and her family, the issues of the day. It was such a deep conversation that I felt it would be important to capture her in this moment of thought.

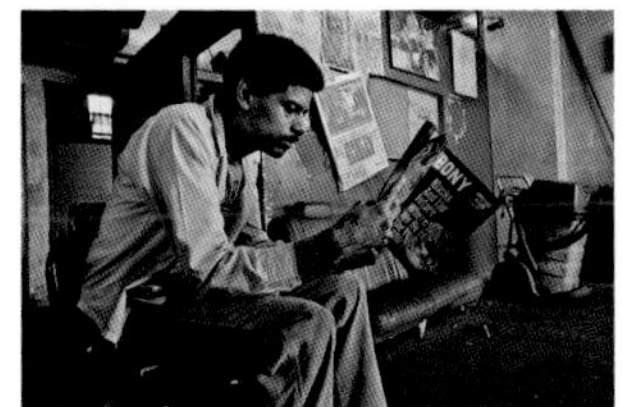
The garage

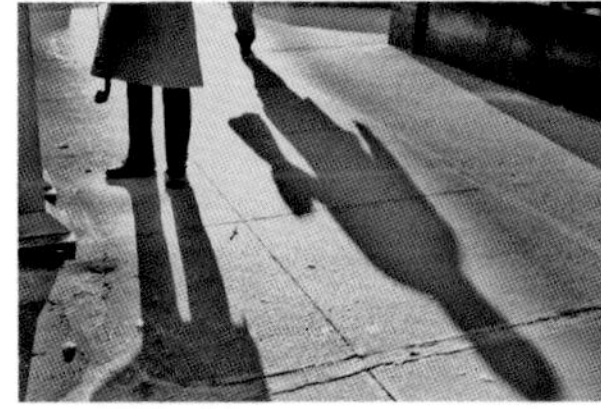
Lunch hour, Kips Bay

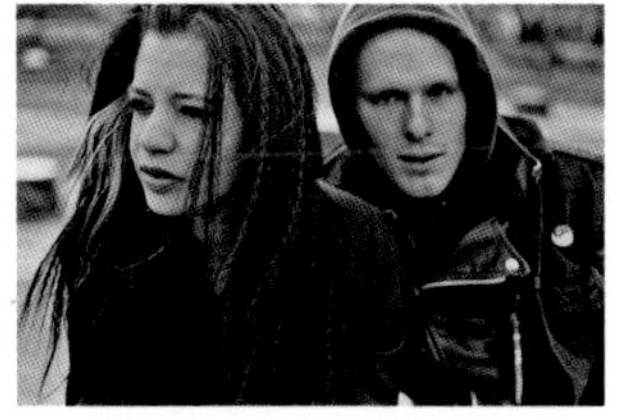
Union Square

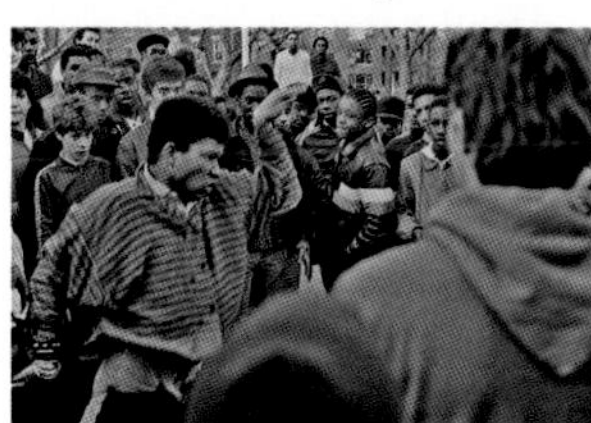
Washington Square, the battle

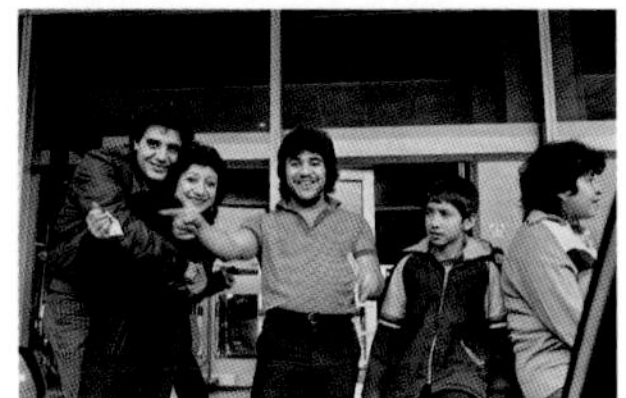
Midtown

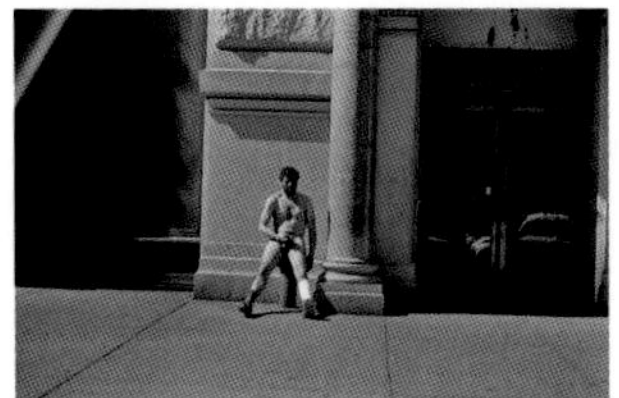
Greenwich Village

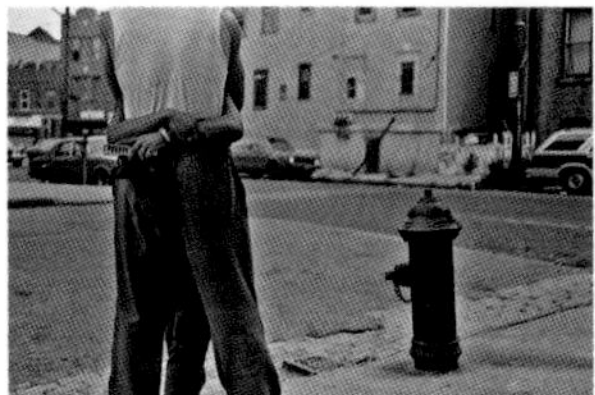
Staten Island

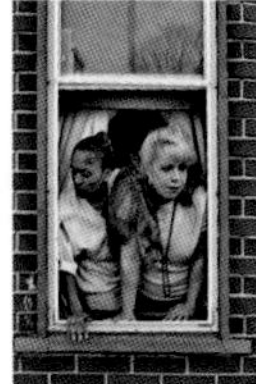
Park Slope

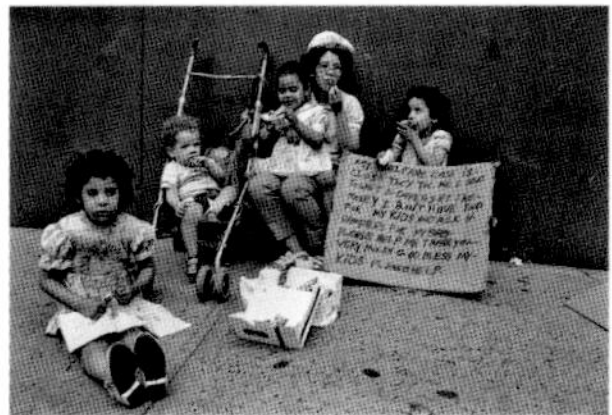

Homeless family, Manhattan

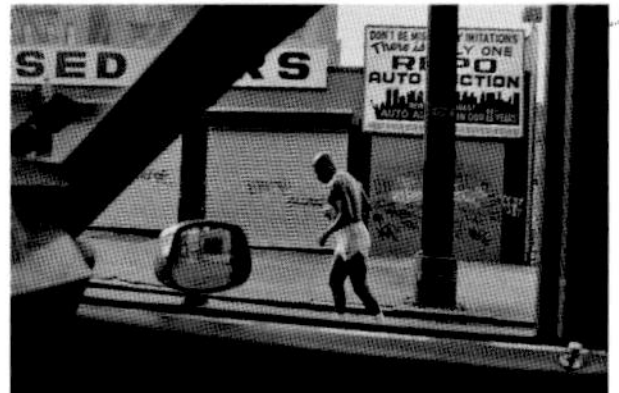

The Bronx

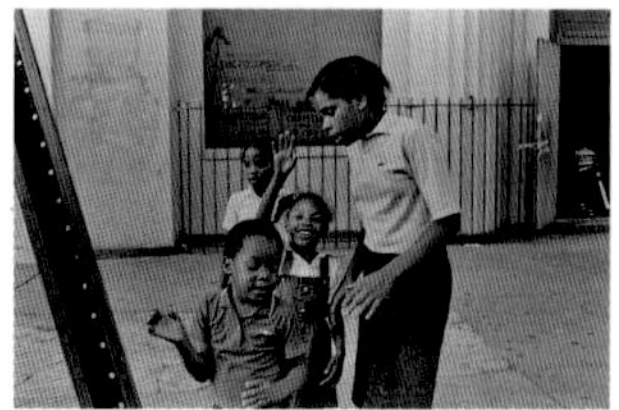

Harlem

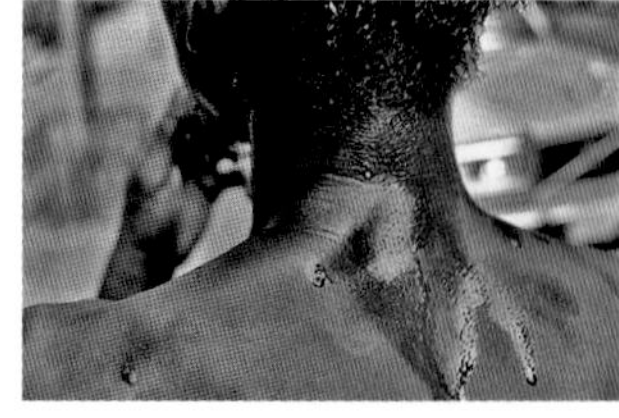

Chelsea

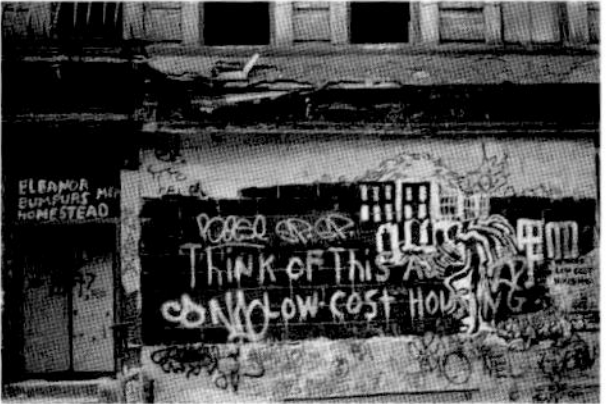

East Village

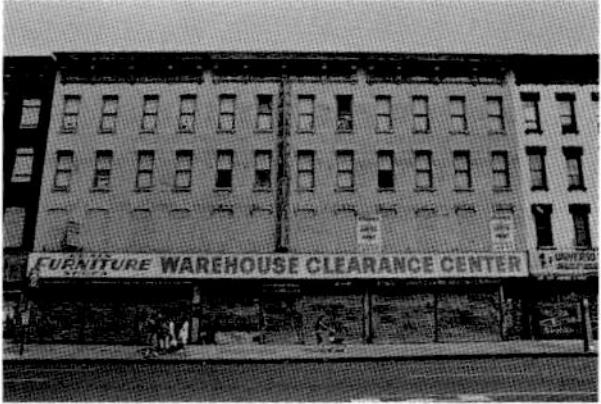

East Harlem

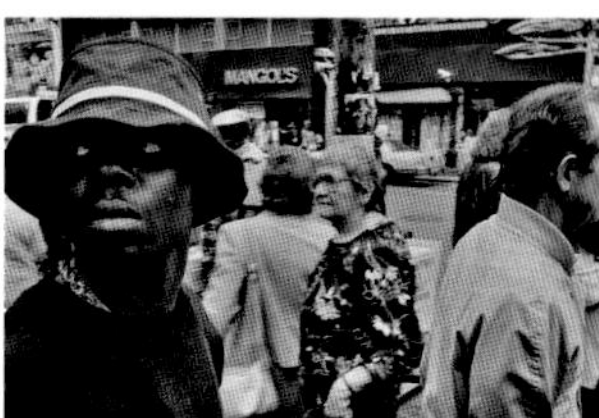

Lexington & 59th Street, Midtown

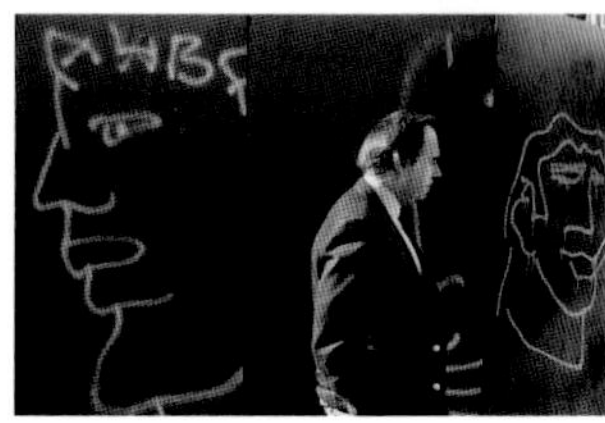

Midtown

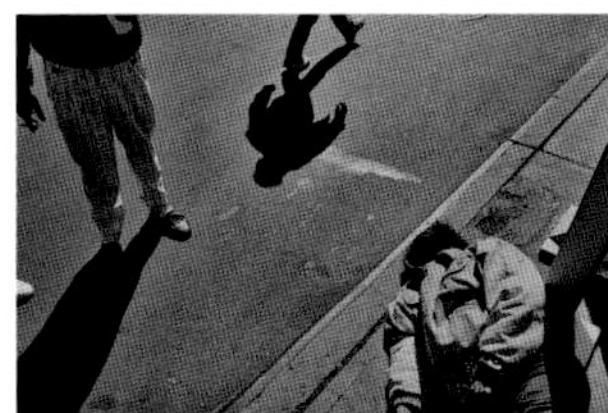

Near the Port Authority Bus Terminal, Midtown

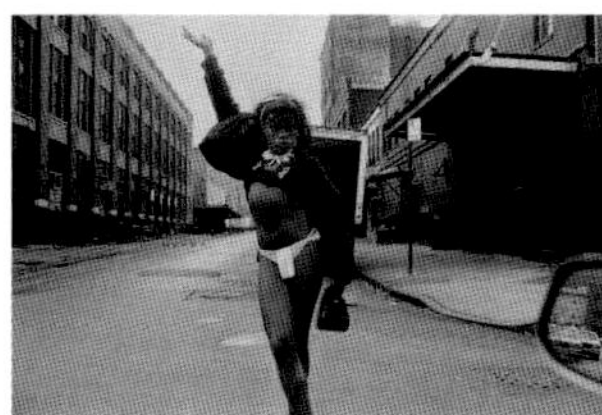

Meatpacking District, Greenwich Village

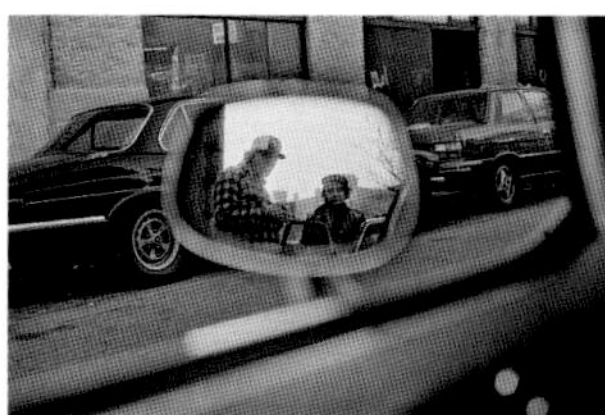

Outside a West Houston after-hours club waiting for a fare

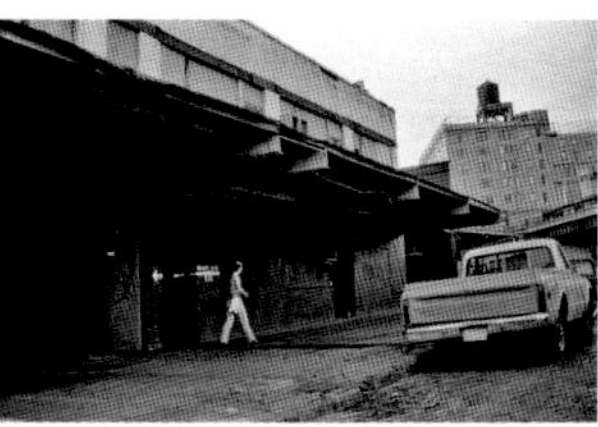

Waiting for a fare early Sunday morning in front of the Mineshaft, a BDSM club in the Meatpacking District

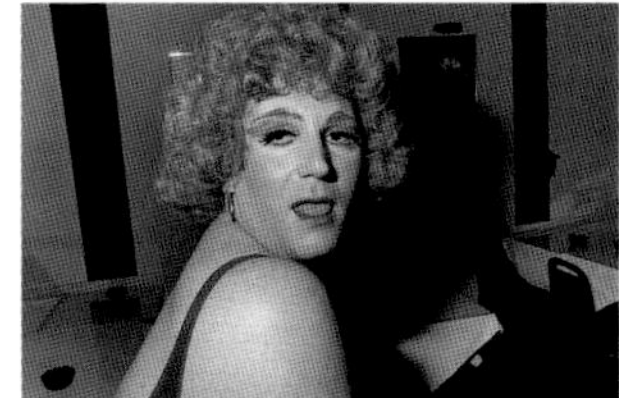

The Fabric Factory, Times Square

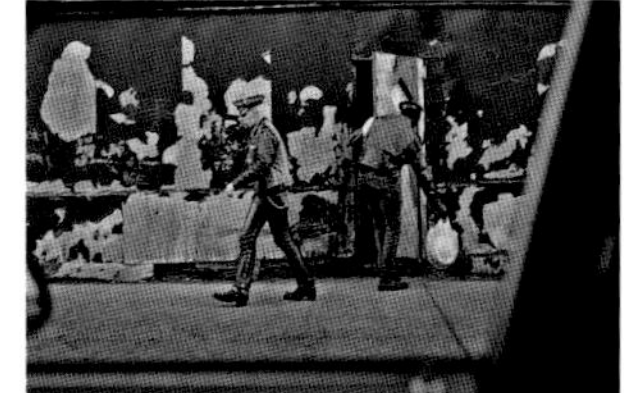

Outside the Vault, a popular S&M club. This was probably about 9 a.m.; some are going in, some are coming out.

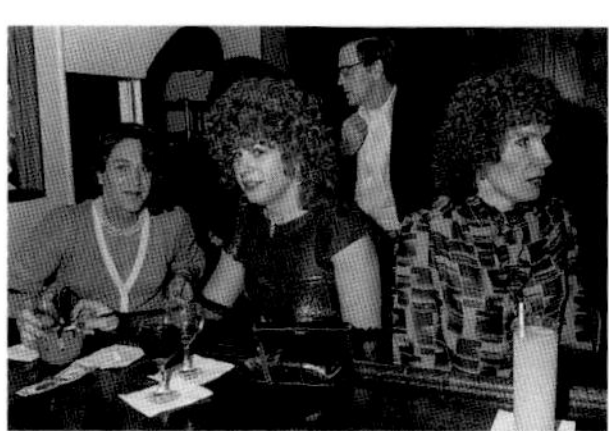

The Fabric Factory, Times Square

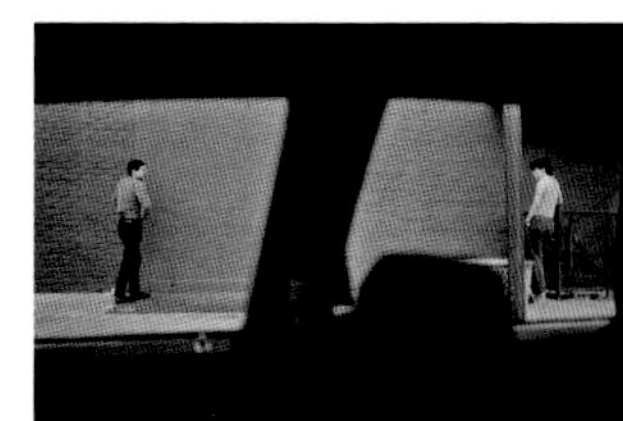

14th Street & West Side Highway. That's the back of the Anvil. These guys would come outside to take a leak. And of course they're having a conversation, so who knows what happened after that.

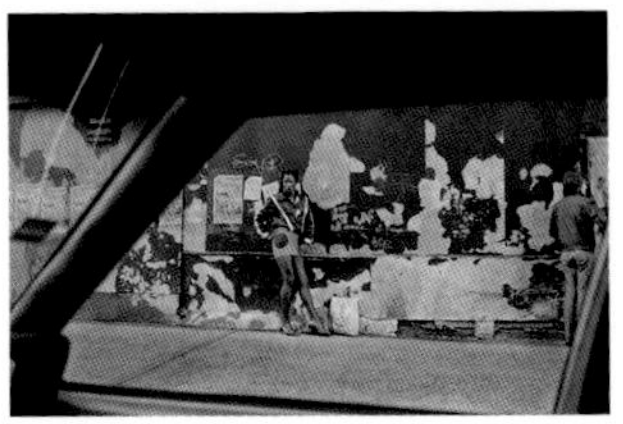
Chelsea

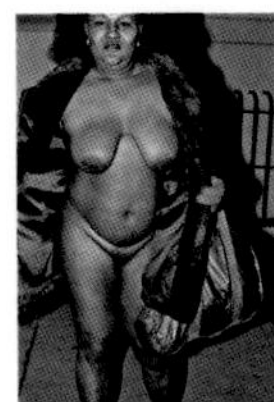
Untitled

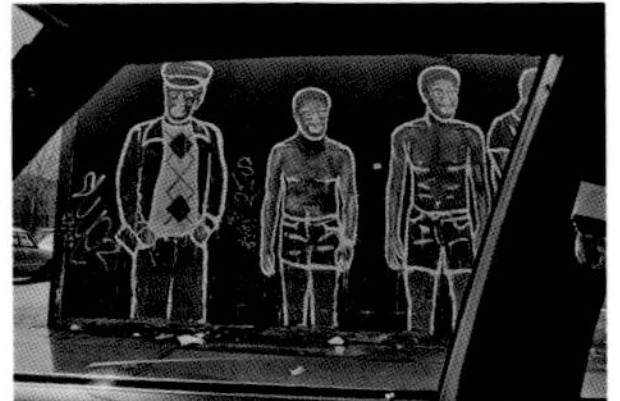
Delancey Street, Lower East Side. The artist Robert Goldman was a co-founder of the activist arts organization ABC No Rio.

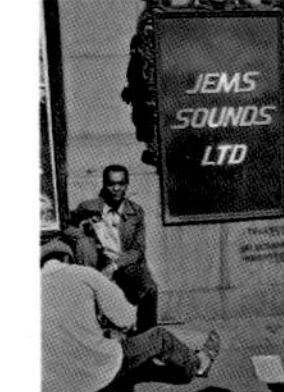

Midtown

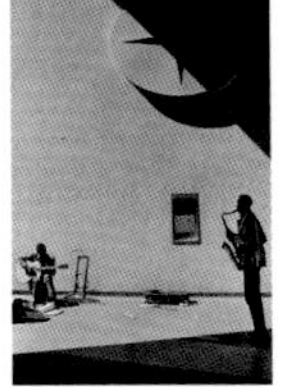
Citicorp Building, Midtown

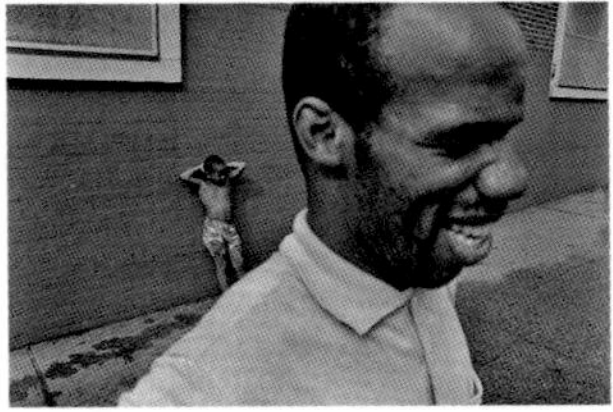
East Harlem

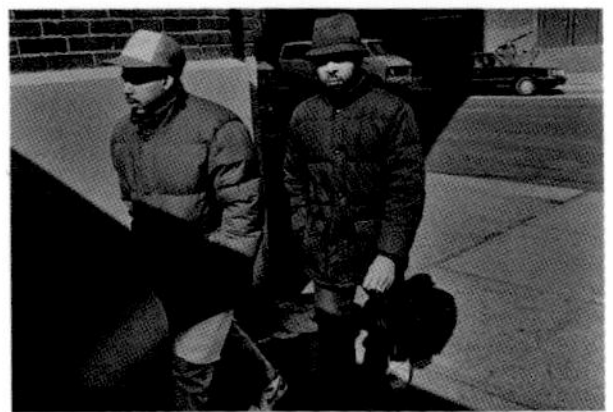
Greenwich Village

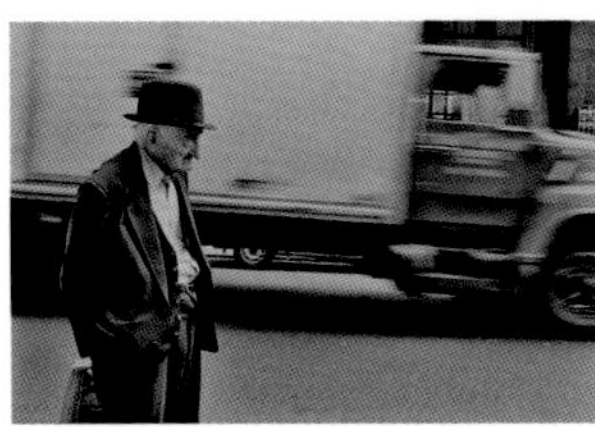
Kips Bay

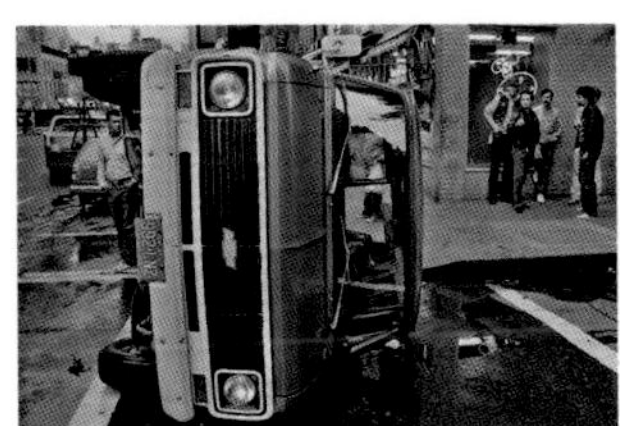
Car accident

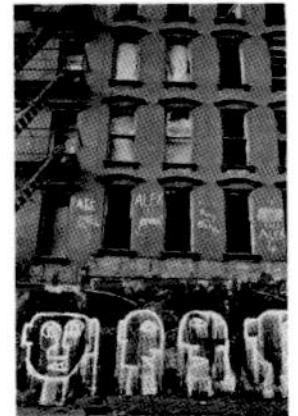
East Village, that whole neighborhood looked like this back then. The graffiti is by Luca Pizzorno, an Italian artist who died because of AIDS in the mid-90s.

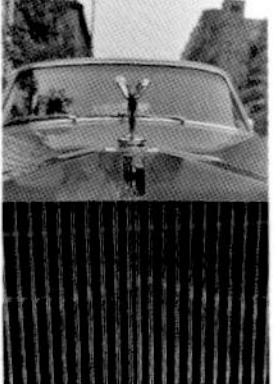
Upper East Side

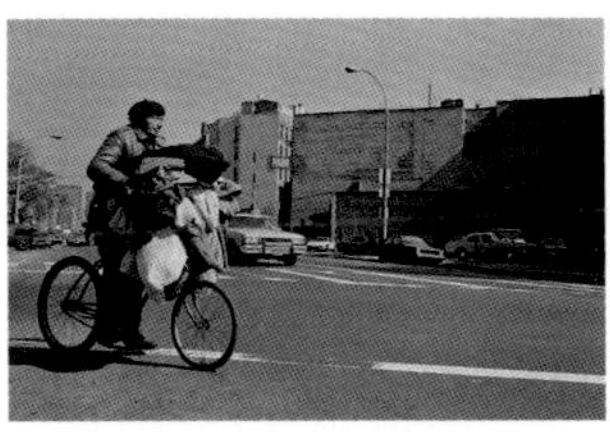
Bowery & East 4th Street, East Village

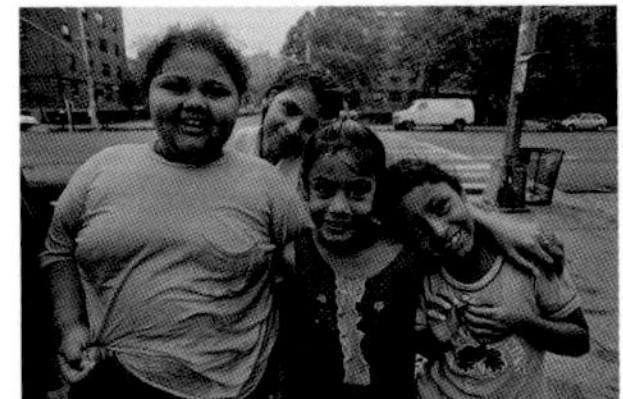
East Harlem

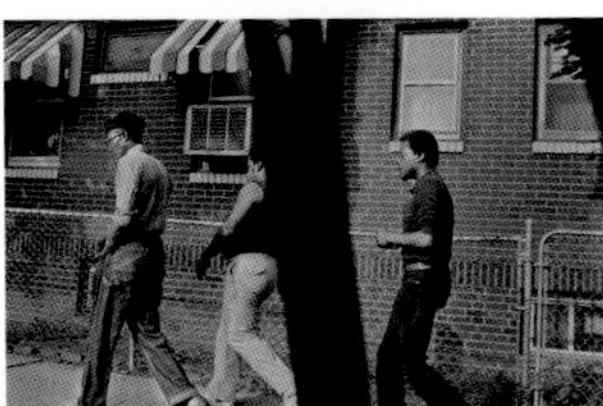
North Conduit Boulevard, Queens

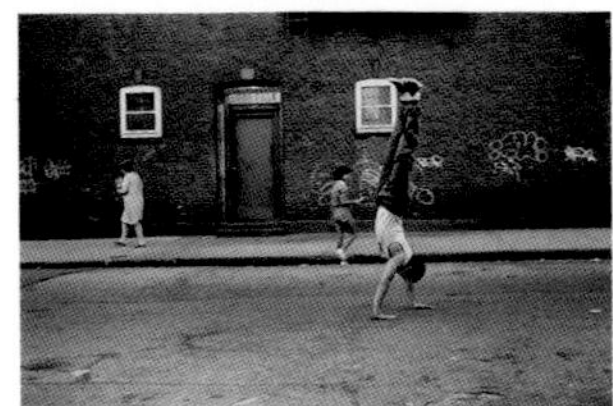
Staten Island

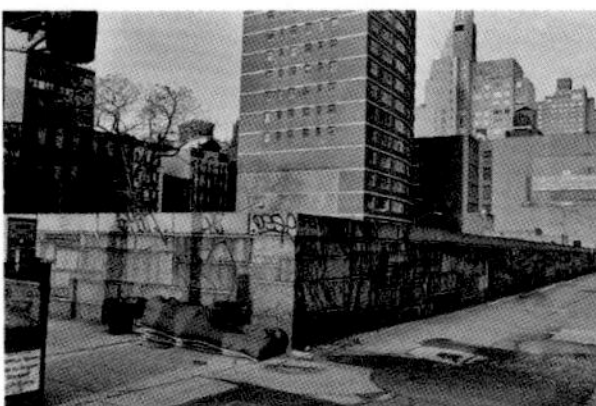
Midtown Tunnel

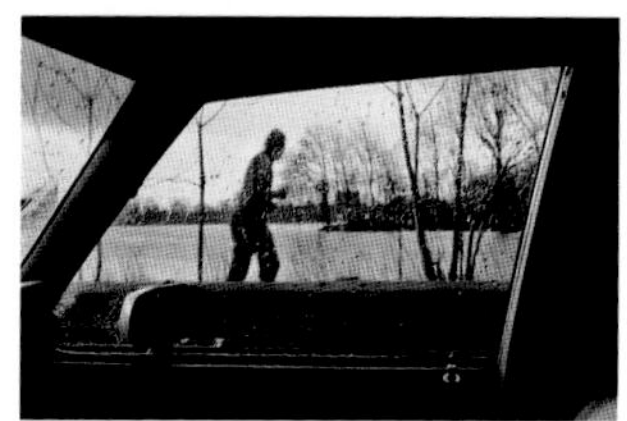

Central Park

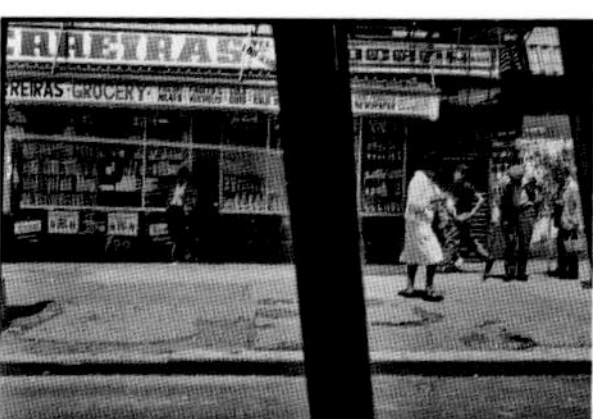

East Harlem

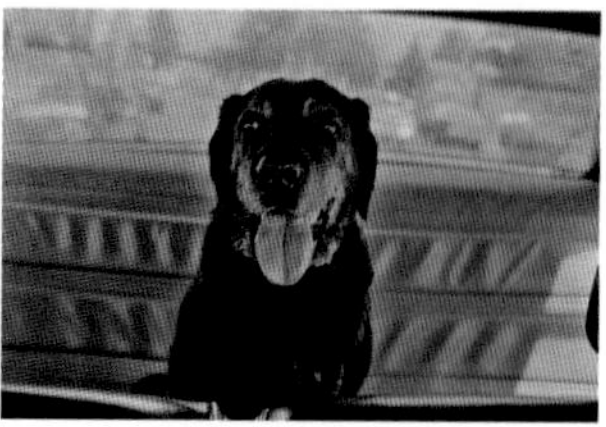

Untitled

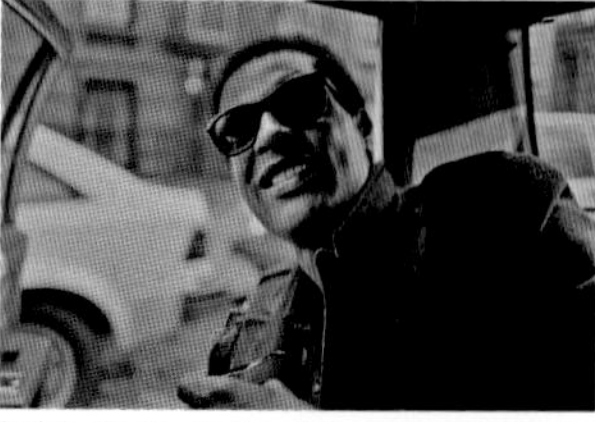

I picked him up at a club and I took him to Brooklyn. He was a happy camper.

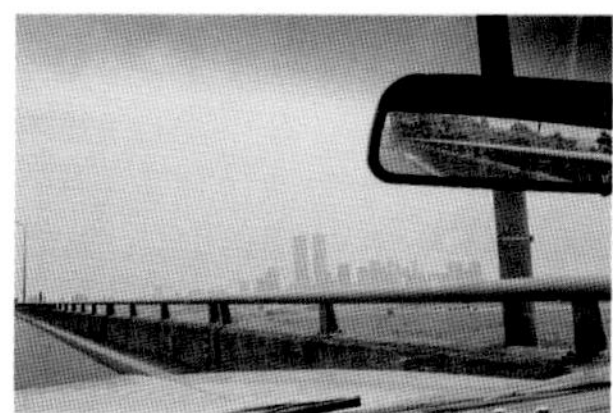

New Jersey

JOSEPH RODRÍGUEZ is a documentary photographer born and raised in Brooklyn, New York. He studied photography at the School of Visual Arts and in the Photojournalism and Documentary Photography Program at the International Center of Photography in New York City.

Recent exhibitions of his work have appeared at Galleri Kontrast, Stockholm, Sweden; The African American Museum, Philadelphia, Pennsylvania; The Fototeca, Havana, Cuba; Birmingham Civil Rights Institute, Birmingham, Alabama; Open Society Institute's Moving Walls, New York, New York; Frieda and Roy Furman Gallery at the Walter Reade Theater at the Lincoln Center, New York, New York; and the Kari Kenneti Gallery, Helsinki, Finland.

In 2001 the Juvenile Justice website, featuring Joseph Rodriguez's photographs, launched in partnership with the Human Rights Watch International Film Festival High School Pilot Program.

Rodríguez teaches at New York University, the International Center of Photography, New York, and has also taught at universities in Mexico and Europe.

He won an Alicia Patterson Journalism Fellowship in 1993 photographing gang families in East Los Angeles.

RICHARD PRICE is the author of several novels, including *Clockers*, *Freedomland*, and *Samaritan*. He won a 2007 Edgar Award for his writing on the HBO series *The Wire*.

ANDY OUTIS is a graphic designer and creative director working in New York City. He began his creative career as a graffiti artist in the San Francisco Bay Area, and is a graduate of the MFA Design Program at the School of Visual Arts.

TAXI: Journey Through My Windows 1977–1987

Published in the United States by powerHouse Books,
a division of powerHouse Cultural Entertainment, Inc.
32 Adams Street, Brooklyn, NY 11201-1021
e-mail: info@powerHouseBooks.com
website: www.powerHouseBooks.com

First edition, 2020

Library of Congress Control Number: 2019941655

ISBN 978-1-57687-931-3

Designed by Andy Outis
Printed by Artron Art (Group) Co., Ltd

10 9 8 7 6 5 4 3 2 1

Printed and bound in China